TRANSFORM
YOUR LIFE WITH
COLOUR

TRANSFORM
YOUR LIFE WITH
COLOUR

EMOTIONAL, SPIRITUAL AND PHYSICAL
WELLBEING THROUGH COLOUR

charles phillips

LONDON NEW YORK

Published in 2015 by CICO Books
an imprint of Ryland Peters & Small Ltd
20–21 Jockey's Fields, London WC1R 4BW

www.rylandpeters.com

10 9 8 7 6 5 4 3 2 1

First published as *Colour For Life* by Ryland Peters
& Small in 2004

Text © Ryland Peters & Small 2004
Design © CICO Books 2015

A CIP catalogue record for this book is available from the
British Library.

ISBN: 978 1 78249 207 8

Printed in China

Editor: Henrietta Heald
Designer: Emily Breen

In-house editor: Dawn Bates
In-house designer: Fahema Khanam
Art director: Sally Powell
Production: Patricia Harrington
Publishing manager: Penny Craig
Publisher: Cindy Richards

contents

introduction

Every day of our lives we are affected by color. The decorative scheme in a room can quicken our spirits; the bright shades of sportswear can boost our energy levels; the food colors on our plates at mealtimes can stimulate appetite. Outdoors, a bank of yellow daffodils in a spring garden may touch us with delight, or the reds and oranges of autumnal trees amaze us.

Natural daylight contains the colors of the spectrum that we see displayed in the rainbow that sometimes follows a storm. Our moods and physiological responses are affected by the different combinations of spectrum colors in daylight at various times of the day and in the different seasons of the year. For example, compare your mood in the yellow light of a sunny afternoon with how you feel in the mauve dusk or indigo midnight a few hours later; think of how your energy levels dip as the hours of daylight shorten with the approach of winter, but pick up again with the different color mix of the longer days of spring.

Colors have a powerful impact, speaking directly to us all on a level deep beneath conscious thought. The colors we choose for our clothing at work and play and for our decorative schemes at home tell other people a great deal about us. Depending on our natural coloring, there are some colors that each of us should avoid; equally, some colors send out messages about us that we may not wish to broadcast. Often the effect is more powerful because it is unspoken.

The language of color is one we all hear but often cannot speak—we feel its effects without being able to explain them. Nevertheless, as we become attuned to color, we learn to use it to present ourselves and our homes to best advantage. In this book you will find accessible advice on combining colors in your living room or kitchen, on creating a beautiful spread of colors in your garden, on the best colors to wear for an important job interview or dinner date, on the links between food color and nutritional value, and on the connections between color and health.

For color also influences physical, psychological, and spiritual vitality. The powerful effects of color vibrations embrace the body and open doorways to the mind and spirit; they can be used to boost and safeguard physical health and to soothe or enliven the soul. The therapeutic use of colored gems, color-vitalized drinks, and colored light derives from time-honored wisdom that can be traced back at least as far as ancient Egypt and also finds expression in Indian Ayurvedic medicine. Each one of us is unique. Finding and using the right colors for you can enhance your spiritual growth, boost your self-esteem, help you to overcome fears and mental obstacles, and unleash your creativity.

the *meaning* of *color*

light and *pigments*

You cannot tell your red socks and blue socks apart in a pitch-dark bedroom because you cannot see color without light. Color is carried by light. Indeed, color is light. What we perceive as red is light of a particular wavelength and frequency, while blue is light of a different wavelength and frequency. Light and color are the way humans experience one part of the electromagnetic spectrum.

RAINBOW COLORS

The rainbow colors are combined in sunlight. In 1666 the English scientist Isaac Newton revealed the constituent colors of sunlight by passing rays through a glass prism and producing the spectrum of colors: red–orange–yellow–green–blue–indigo–violet. The reason why these colors appear in the rainbow after a storm is that droplets of water in the atmosphere function as tiny prisms, splitting the rays of light.

ELECTROMAGNETIC RADIATION

We are bombarded by waves of electromagnetic energy from the sun and other stars, and from terrestrial sources. But visible light is only one-sixtieth of the full range of electromagnetic radiation.

At one end of the spectrum are radio and television waves, microwaves and radar waves, all of which are long waves with a slow frequency of vibration.

At the other end of the spectrum are gamma waves, which are short waves vibrating at a fast frequency.

Infrared waves of light are just too long for humans to see, but can be felt as heat.

The visible colors in sunlight range from red (the longest wave we can see) through the other colors of the rainbow—orange, yellow, green, blue and indigo—to violet (the shortest wave we can see).

Just beyond our vision at the short-wave end of the spectrum are ultraviolet rays, then x-rays and gamma rays.

REFLECTED LIGHT

When we see an object in a particular color, we are registering the wavelength of light that the object reflects. A red chair, for example, absorbs all the wavelengths of visible light except the red ones. A blackboard absorbs all colors, while a brilliant white door reflects all the colors of visible white light. An object will appear to be a different color under colored light.

MIXING COLORS

White light can be split into just three primary colors: red-orange, green, and blue-violet. If you train three spotlights in these colors on a theater stage, you create a white beam. This process is known as additive mixing. The colors in paints and fabrics are made in a different way—by subtractive mixing. In this context the three primary colors are red, blue, and yellow. They cannot be made by mixing other colors. When they are combined, the product is black.

HIGH-AMPLITUDE COLORS

A bright blue or bright yellow is exciting to the eye—just a small brightly painted area may be enough to enliven an entire room, and a small accent such as a buttonhole flower can transform a formal suit.

A color appears brighter when it is reflected strongly and when it has a tall wavelength (a larger distance between the high point and the low point of the wave). Colors with tall wavelengths are said in the jargon to have "high amplitude."

how we see *color*

People with normal sight can identify colors without conscious effort. The colors in light are distinguished by the retina at the rear of the eye. When light rays enter the eye, they pass through the cornea and then through a watery fluid known as the aqueous humour before reaching the lens. The light rays are focused by the lens onto the retina, where they stimulate two specialized cells—rods and cones.

Rods are highly sensitive to light but not to color. They can distinguish between shades of gray, white, and black, enabling us to make things out in poor light. Cones come in three types, each holding a pigment that absorbs one of the three different wavelengths of light: long wavelength (red/orange), middle wavelength (green), and short wavelength (blue/violet). When it comes into contact with light of the wavelength to which it is sensitive, the pigment breaks down, and this process sends an impulse along the optic nerve on the start of its journey to the brain, where it is interpreted.

If light of more than one wavelength enters the eye, more than one type of cone is stimulated. If you see a man in a yellow shirt, the light rays stimulate a mixture of cones sensitive to red and green light—and the signals sent by the cones deliver a message interpreted by the brain as "yellow." People who are colorblind have abnormal numbers of cones sensitive to particular light wavelengths—so they cannot see those colors as other people do.

"SEEING" COLORS THROUGH THE SKIN
Some blind people are capable of distinguishing between paper or cloth of different colors simply by holding their fingertips or hands above the pieces of material. They can feel the different wavelengths of light through their skin—and report that some colors feel cool while others are warm.

You may find that you can train yourself to experience this phenomenon. Take some squares of colored cloth and lay them on a table. Pass your hands over the squares with your eyes shut. Be sensitive to any differences in energy you can feel. Over many days, perhaps a few weeks, repeat the experiment and see if you can develop an association between types of energy field and particular colors.

the *wheel* of *colors*

Color therapists—who use colored light and materials for healing—teach that we each have a "soul color" that appeals to us very strongly and feeds our spirit. Equally, we all acknowledge colors or color combinations that do not make us feel good. Indeed, they may "turn us off," making us feel ill at ease or even physically unwell—perhaps because they recall an unpleasant experience or simply because we do not like their vibrational energy.

In addition to our highly personal color likes and dislikes, we all share recognition of certain color combinations that work well and others that clash. The color wheel is a traditional tool for determining which colors complement one another and which ones are likely to produce a jarring effect.

A color wheel is made by joining the two ends of the color spectrum—red and violet—at a point on a circle and running the colors of the spectrum around the circle's circumference. The three primary colors from which all pigments are made—red, yellow, and blue—sit at one-third intervals on the circle.

ONE, TWO, THREE

The color that sits at the halfway point on the circumference between two primaries is known as a secondary color. The secondary that falls halfway between red and yellow is orange. The other secondary colors are green, halfway between yellow and blue, and violet, the mid-point between blue and red.

The color that is found halfway between a primary color and its secondary is called a tertiary color. The tertiary between yellow (primary) and green (secondary) is a bright lime green.

The colors opposite each another on the color wheel are called complementaries. The complementary color to red is green, while orange is complementary to blue, and yellow is complementary to violet. These colors "attract" one another and can makea pleasing combination in an outfit, a decorative scheme, or a bank of flowers. Each color draws out the richness of the other. Imagine a box of oranges packed in blue tissue—the packaging makes the orange color of the fruit much more striking.

COLORS OF LIGHT

The color wheel described above is based on the colors in pigments and dyes. Healers and color therapists working with colored light draw up a different color wheel built around the three primary colors red/orange, green, and blue/violet. On this wheel the complementary of red/orange is turquoise, the complementary of green is magenta, and the complementary of blue/violet is orange/yellow. Colored light treatments use both a color and its complementary (see page 128).

(see page 128)

TYPES OF COLOR SCHEME

The traditional theory of colors defines several harmonious "color schemes"—combinations of colors that look good.

A complementary color scheme uses opposites on the wheel—for example, blue furnishings and accents with burnt-orange walls.

A monochromatic scheme uses a single color in many different shades—dark blue, sky blue, royal blue and so on.

An analogous scheme uses colors that are adjacent on the wheel—yellow with lime green or blue with blue-violet.

An achromatic scheme uses black, white, silver, and gray; it may need enlivening with accents of bright color from other groups—for example, a minimalist black-and-white interior might be improved by a dramatic red rug.

TRADITIONAL COLOR WHEEL

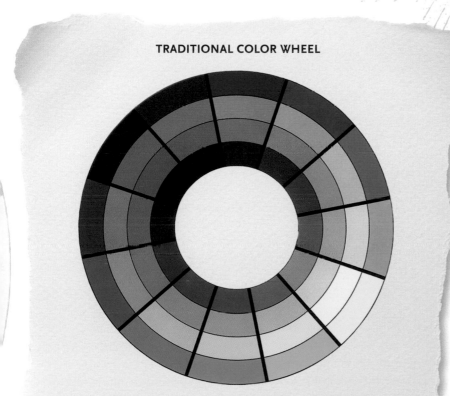

Primary	Secondary	Tertiary	Complementary
red	orange	red–orange, orange–yellow	green
yellow	green	yellow–green, blue–green	violet
blue	violet	violet–blue, violet–red	orange

your *colors*

Each of us has a particular coloring—a natural "color scheme" consisting of the colors of our eyes, skin, and hair. These colors may be inherited from our parents or—having skipped a generation, thanks to a non-dominant or "recessive" gene—from one of our grandparents. Other factors can also play a part. If you are raised in a Mediterranean climate, for example, your residual skin coloring will grow darker and your hair may bleach from prolonged exposure to sunlight. Illness, too, can affect your complexion and hair color. My grandmother went gray overnight as a result of a serious illness when she was a young woman in the 1920s.

But our attractions to particular colors go far beyond a conscious decision to be in harmony with our hair or skin coloring. We are drawn to colors on an instinctive level, perhaps because they express something powerful and non-verbal about our personality and approach to life.

COLOR'S HELP IN TIME OF NEED

In addition to having a permanent preference for a color scheme, we may feel drawn to particular colors at times of exhaustion, stress, or emotional need. We need the boost of a particular color vibration to correct our body's balance of energies. At the simplest level, we all feel the effect of putting on bright party clothes—perhaps in vivid red, lordly purple, or glittering silver or gold—which enliven us even if we are tired or lethargic. If you are working at home for a day and can choose where to settle down, you may find yourself choosing one room over another because of the interaction between its color scheme and your mood. If you have to cope with a bereavement or shock, you may seek solace in green, the soothing color of the heart, perhaps by going for country walks or wearing a comfortable green slicker or scarf. At this and similar times you are drawn to the vibrational energy of one color above others.

Equally, you may have a strong reaction against a color, indicating that you are overloaded with that color's vibration—you will benefit from incorporating its complementary color into your life (see pages 14–15). For example, if you feel a strong negative response to orange at a particular time, find something blue to look at or wear—or buy a blue hanging to put in your home. Develop your sensitivity to your body's responses to color and follow your instincts.

YOUR NATURAL COLORS

Our natural coloring usually has a powerful influence on the colors we prefer to wear.

people with fair or blond hair, who usually have green, blue, or gray eyes are generally attracted by the colors green or blue.

people with brown eyes and dark hair/complexion often choose rich, bright colors.

red-headed people are another group who tend to like blues and greens.

GET TO KNOW YOURSELF BETTER

If you have a strong preference for a particular color, you are likely to have the characteristics associated with that color.

red
extrovert, excitable, sensuous, passionate, full of energy

orange
independent-minded, strong-willed, a self-starter

green
sensitive, observant, diplomatic, caring and careful

yellow
capable, quick-witted, spontaneous, confident, a good communicator

blue
creative, imaginative, deep-feeling, sincere

purple
compassionate, intuitive, with high standards

white
broadminded, a perfectionist, optimistic, self-sufficient

black
self-disciplined, full of opinions, independent, possessing inner strength

changing *colors*

We all have a vital and subtle connection to color in the world around us, seeing colors differently as the quality of light changes at various times of the day and night. On a day of rest or illness, you may have watched the effects of changing daylight on the wall of your room—and perhaps noticed how at different times the colors in your curtains or rug appear to vary under the influence of a light in which different colors predominate.

Imagine being a silent witness for a 24-hour span in a summer garden. Think of the pale, bluish light just before sunrise and the warmer, yellowish colors of afternoon sunlight. Consider the purple-violet shadows and milky whiteness of the scene bathed peacefully in moonlight.

PRESIDING COLORS

Being attuned to the presiding or ruling color at a particular time of day can help us to feel a deeper personal harmony and a more intimate integration with the outside world. In the dawn light, blue is predominant. As the morning progresses, blue shades through turquoise into darker greens. Around the middle of the day, the green light begins to turn yellow. Throughout the afternoon, yellow darkens, becoming a rich reddish-orange by early evening. As the evening progresses, orange light becomes red and then turns to mauve. Mauve shifts into magenta, and in the midnight hours magenta becomes a rich purple. About halfway between midnight and dawn, purple is overtaken by violet.

Those of us living in northern latitudes are affected by these different light vibrations even in the winter months, when we spend a great deal of time in darkness.

SEASONAL COLORS

A parallel cycle of color change can be traced through the seasons. Winter, spring, summer, fall—each has its own unmistakable energy flow and collection of colors.

A winter landscape is often one of stark contrasts—a bare black tree silhouetted against a pale sky, or a dark-looking, twiggy hedge dissecting a snow-covered field. Bright berries or dark evergreen leaves stand out all the more clearly against frosty ground or the chilly white-gray of winter clouds.

In spring, green shoots rise and the whites, pastel pinks, and blues of blossoms delight the eye. We look out for banks of yellow daffodils.

Summer suggests the golden yellows of sunshine and crops, the pale blues of the cloudless sky and the sea that restlessly reflects it, with lavender and the pinks of flowers.

In fall, rich colors come to the fore—the russet brown, gold, earthy red, and orange of falling leaves and the mellow, burnished crops that are carried in from the fields.

SEASONAL PERSONALITIES

The color theorist Johannes Itten, an artist who worked at the Bauhaus school of design, architecture, and arts in Germany, developed the theory that people fall into one of four seasonal types depending on whether their natural coloring belongs to winter, spring, summer, or fall. Itten noticed that his art students were attracted to colors that were attuned to their seasonal type. Later theorists developed and elaborated these observations, identifying particular traits of character that could be associated with different seasonal types.

WHAT SEASONAL TYPE ARE YOU?

Color theorists suggest that each of the different seasonal types has typical associated personality traits.

winter type
Dark brown or black hair; brown, black, or green eyes; brown, olive, or beige complexion. Winter personalities are responsible and self-possessed, with natural authority and a will to get things done; you may need to fight an impulse to be impatient with others and be careful not to dismiss efforts that fall short of your standards.

spring type
Golden-brown or blond hair; hazel, green, or blue-gray eyes; a light, peach-colored complexion. Spring personalities are extrovert, charming, and caring, with a lively sense of fun. They may take on too much at once and risk becoming disorganized.

summer type
Light brown or light blond hair; gray-brown, gray, or pale misty blue eyes; a smooth, light complexion. If you are a summer personality, you are a gentle soul and a sensitive listener who is strong on cooperation, analysis, and organization. Good at making and keeping the peace, you may sometimes appear withdrawn or aloof.

fall type
Red, copper, or strawberry-blond hair; brown or green eyes; a copper or dark golden complexion. Fall personalities are warm and lively, and strong thinkers with a well-developed sense of justice and a healthy disregard for convention. They can be moody and may sometimes be accused of being bossy.

colors in *nature*

Color has a vital role to play in the natural world. Plants and animals depend on the cycles and colors of natural light to regulate their growth and behavior from day to day and from season to season. Creatures are guided in their movements and appetites by the passage from the purple-violet hours of night to the blue light of dawn, and the ensuing changes in the predominant colors of light during the day (see pages 18–19). As fall draws to a close, the shortening hours of daylight prepare the plant and animal kingdoms for the winter regime, while the combination of colors in the longer days after the end of winter make possible the regeneration of spring.

ANIMAL COLORS

Color also serves as a vibrant language in the animal kingdom. The wasp wears its distinctive yellow-and-black-striped coloring as a warning to predators and other creatures to stay away. Red or yellow/black is often a signal of danger among fish, insects, and plants. Brilliant colors in fish or bird plumage are used to differentiate the sexes and attract a mate. But these colors may appear different to various species.

NIGHT HUNTERS

Cats, owls, foxes, and other nighttime hunters have highly developed night vision. They can see longer wavelengths of light than humans, including the infrared waves we experience as heat. Being able to "see" heat helps a cat track hidden prey—and this ability also explains why cats always find the warmest place in the home. But cats have less developed vision in the field of colors seen by humans. They see blue and green and a little red, but not very clearly.

UNDERWATER SONG

Apart from apes, the majority of mammals have less developed color vision than humans. But they have enhanced sensitivity in other regions of the electromagnetic spectrum—for example, many have very acute hearing. Male humpback whales communicate by singing songs at very low frequencies that travel great distances underwater. These songs, believed to be part of the mating ritual, can last for 30 minutes each.

LIGHT AND NAVIGATION

A clear sky contains a well-ordered pattern of polarized light. Humans cannot see it, but—according to latest scientific thinking—birds, fish, and even dung beetles use it for navigation. Polarized light is light that vibrates in a single plane, whereas normal light rays have random multidirectional vibrations.

A NEW COLOR DIMENSION

Most birds, bees, and other animals experience color quite differently from humans. Bees and many other insects, for example, are sensitive to ultraviolet light, the short-wavelength colors that are beyond the range of the human eye. Scientists suspect that bees can see ultraviolet guidelines that lead them to pollen in flowers.

In humans, color sensations are generated when light stimulates a combination of three types of cone in the eye (see page 12). But some creatures—including birds, some fish, and turtles—have four types of cone, enabling them to see a wider range of colors and also giving them a different experience of the colors visible to humans. Since this is beyond our experience, we can only imagine what the colors of this new dimension must look like.

Birds, too, can see ultraviolet light. Scientists have found that certain seeds, flowers, and fruits stand out from background vegetation much more clearly in ultraviolet wavelengths than in human-wavelength colors. Humans appreciate the variety of brilliant colors in bird plumage. The birds themselves may see far more than us—tiny differences that we miss, for example in the feathers of male and female blue tits, are much more clearly visible at ultraviolet wavelengths.

ways with *color*

Colors have deep-seated symbolic associations that feed into our responses to clothes, plants, decorative schemes, and the play of light. Some of these color meanings cross the boundaries of language and culture, representing a shared bank of memories that go back to our distant ancestors; others appear to be specific to certain locations and cultures.

Red, the color of blood, symbolizes life itself. In many places, red suggests the earth and the sun at sunrise and sunset. It also has connotations of accessible sexuality—prostitutes have traditionally advertised their services with a red light and were sometimes called "scarlet women." The color's associations with spilt blood mean that red is also sometimes suggestive of violence and warfare. In Ghana, red is a color of death—mourners wear red to honor the memory of a dead relative.

In Western cultures, white has well-established associations with purity and virginity, as seen in the bridal dress and veil. The color suggests the milky light of the moon, and derives some of its virginal associations from its connection to Artemis, a Greek moon goddess who was a fierce defender of sexual purity. In China, however, white is linked with death and is the color of the mourning shroud. A bride who wore a white dress would be bringing unhappiness upon herself; instead she wears red, the Chinese color of happiness. In many cultures, white is held to be a sacred color (see page 24).

Blue is linked with the sky and water. The Roman sky god Jupiter and his goddess–spouse Juno were associated with blue. It is said to be the color of love, and a bride traditionally carries a blue item on her wedding day. Blue is also linked to sincerity, religious faith, hopefulness, and a clear conscience.

Green is associated with healing, balance, and the natural world. In the folk tradition of central and northern Europe, the Green Man personifies nature's creative powers. He appears in art and as an architectural feature, often with a face made of foliage or with leaves and shoots coming out of his mouth, ears, and eyes.

Yellow, the color of fallen leaves, has autumnal connections. In Egypt it was traditionally the color of mourning; at one time, widows in the Brittany region of France wore yellow caps as a sign that they had been touched by death. It also has associations with cowardice and betrayal; in France, national traitors had their doors daubed with yellow paint as a mark of shame. In the Christian tradition, Judas Iscariot, the betrayer of

Christ, is usually depicted in yellow robes. Yellow is also linked with sickness–yellowing skin can be a sign of illness, and yellow was traditionally used to mark an area of quarantine. But rich yellows may be connected with sunlight, joyful vitality, and strength. Christ's disciple Peter is frequently shown in rich yellow robes. In ancient China, yellow was the imperial color, and the doorway to the emperor's palace was called the "yellow door."

Traditionally linked with power and a prominent position in society, purple was a favorite color of the Egyptian queen Cleopatra. It was also the color worn by Roman emperors. Before synthetic purple dye was developed in the 19th century, natural purple dye was very expensive. In ancient times, "royal" or "imperial" purple was laboriously made from the shells of mollusks. Purple is also associated with intuition and imagination–according to color theorists, purple bedroom walls will boost a child's imaginative powers.

In the Western tradition, black is the color of death and mourning, and is linked with evil, magic, and the "dark arts." But black and gray are also the colors traditionally favored by priests, and black is the color of sophisticated formal wear. In ancient Egypt, black was the color of the goddess Isis, and black cats were seen as sacred to the goddess and possessed of holy powers.

COLORS OF THE HEAVENS

The sun, moon, and each of the planets is traditionally associated with a different color and a distinctive quality or influence.

Planet/Body	Color	Planet's Associations
Sun	yellow	linked to Apollo, Greek god of music and poetry
Moon	white	promotes chastity
Mars	red	brings war
Jupiter	blue	brings happiness
Venus	green	presides over love
Mercury	purple	the Roman god Mercury was a messenger and god of trade
Saturn	black	associated with time, and in the astrological tradition an evil planet to be born under

feeling blue–*color* and the *spirit*

Color has tremendous spiritual force. Its energy can stimulate and uplift the soul, while its symbolic meanings enrich religious expression. The powerful associations and inspirational qualities of color inform the world's great religious traditions.

White has been associated with holiness since at least the era of the Persian Zoroastrian religion in the 6th century B.C. In the Judaeo-Christian tradition, white is the color of angels' wings and of the robes worn by Christ after his resurrection. It is also associated with peace–and is the color of the dove chosen by Christians as the image of the Holy Spirit.

Darker shades of blue were the colors of the Mother and Earth Goddess worshipped by ancient pagans; in the Christian tradition, blue was the color linked to the Virgin Mary, mother of Christ, who was taken into the heavens at the Assumption. Christians traditionally hold that a blue cloth draped over a coffin symbolizes immortality. Sky blue has general connotations of spiritual awareness, understanding, and depth of character and is particularly associated with Hindu gods–especially Krishna, one of the incarnations of the god Vishnu. Krishna is represented with light blue skin, which indicates to Hindus that he has the power to overcome evil.

Green is sacred in Islam and was said to be the color of the prophet Muhammad's robe. In Christian imagery, green represents the resurrection of the dead, while pale green is linked with the rite of baptism, in which new church members are blessed with holy water. In both Islam and Christianity, red is associated with the blood of those who sacrificed themselves in the cause of their religion. In India, yellow is often the color of renunciation of worldly appetites–in the Buddhist tradition, monks wear yellow or orange robes–but in the Hindu festival of Holi, bright yellow, red, and other colors are used to celebrate the arrival of spring.

Purple, associated with royalty and secular power, is also a color of intuition and spiritual power. It is the color of bishops' robes in the Christian church, reflecting both their preeminence and spiritual authority. It also has connections with grief and sadness over wrongdoing: some Christian churches are decorated with purple on Ash Wednesday, at the start of Lent; purple also appears on the Saturday of Easter week, the day following Good Friday.

Some religious groups associate gray, black, or brown with a life of moderation, simplicity, and love of others. These colors are chosen by many Christian monastic groups for their robes. Early Quakers chose to wear gray, brown, or black as a sign that they had rejected frippery and chosen a simple life.

COLOR AND MOOD

Which colors represent various moods? The connection between color and mood is well established in everyday language.

blue
Associated with the phrases "feeling blue" and "got the blues," which mean feeling depressed, battered by events, but perhaps with a steely resilience; blues music can give someone an energetic spiritual uplift through keen feeling and expression of sadness.

green
Associated with the phrases "green-eyed monster" or "green with envy," meaning jealous or envious.

yellow
Associated with the phrase "yellow-bellied," meaning cowardly.

red
Associated with the phrase "seeing red," which means getting angry or ready for violence in a flash.

black
Associated with the phrase "a black mood," which means unable to see a way forward or to feel any hope.

color and the *senses*

A scent can lift or depress our whole mood; it can disgust us physically or transport our imagination to a place of brightly colored memories. Our sense of smell and our sense of taste are so closely linked that we can sometimes taste a bad odor. There may also be a mental connection between the senses of smell and sight. Most of us make subconscious associations between odors and colors, and tend to prefer scents that are in harmony with the vibrations of the colors we like.

COLOR AND EVAPORATION IN PERFUMES

Perfume-makers describe the oils they combine in their scents–according to how quickly or slowly the oils evaporate–as "top notes," "middle notes," and "base notes." Top notes are those that evaporate fastest; bottom notes are those that evaporate most slowly. The best perfumes usually contain a blend of top notes, middle notes, and base notes. The range of "notes" in oils can be overlaid on the spectrum of rainbow colors. Base notes have deeper vibrations and align with the longer waves of the red end of the spectrum, while top notes have lighter vibrations and are equivalent to the violet end of the rainbow.

COLOR AND AROMATHERAPY

Aromatherapists who use natural scented oils in healing teach that some scents harmonize with a person's color vibrations while others do not. In particular they will often ask a client which of the rainbow colors she is particularly drawn to at times of crisis or illness, since this may indicate a deficiency in the chakra or energy center associated with that color. (The body's chakras are described on pages 120–121 and page 126.)

SYNESTHESIA

People with the medical condition synesthesia "see" scents or tastes as colors. Medical experts believe that the condition arises when genetic abnormalities cause unusual connections to form between the parts of the brain that receive signals about scent, taste, and color, causing the functions to become entangled. Many of us may imagine a color when we encounter a scent, but people with synaesthesia actually have the sensation of seeing the colors.

There are several types of synesthesia. Some people with the condition experience sounds as colors, while other people see different colors for each letter and word. Artists in many fields have or have had synesthesia. They include the writer Vladimir Nabokov, the artists Wassily Kandinsky and David Hockney, and the composers Franz Liszt and Olivier Messiaen.

ARE YOUR FAVORITE COLORS CONNECTED WITH YOUR FAVORITE SCENTS?

Test the theory that color preferences are closely tied to choice of perfume by comparing your own likes and dislikes against this checklist.

green and rustic brown
your favorite scents may be citrus or earthy

silvery grays and pastel colors
your favorite scents may be flowers and non-citrus fruits

deep green and orange
your favorite scents may be woody

terracotta and red-purple
your favorite scents may be heavily spiced and autumnal

white, black, and cream
your favorite scents may be leather and incense

chapter 2
color and *clothes*

unspoken language

Each day, the clothes you wear send out messages about who you are and the kind of person you aspire to be. You may have a favorite "look"—formal, sporty, country, urban, futuristic, or bohemian—and you probably also adapt your outfit to fit in with your natural skin and hair coloring and your color preferences. The color scheme affects both you yourself and the people around you—the personality your chosen colors represent is a central part of the first impression that you create, whether you are meeting friends, colleagues, family members, acquaintances, or strangers.

COLLECTIVE CONSCIOUSNESS

The zeitgeist, or "spirit of the age," is reflected in color fashions as well as in political and religious attitudes and artistic tastes. Changing fashions in color may reflect our shared psychological needs. For example, the early years of the 21st century have seen an enthusiasm for blue, a calming color believed to boost good communication—perhaps reflecting our unspoken shared understanding that we need to turn away from conflict and talk peace. The popularity of "natural" colors such as leaf green and terracotta reflects widespread concern about environmental issues.

Some major companies—from car manufacturers to interior designers—invest large sums of money in researching which colors and color combinations will become fashionable. The taste for blue will, they say, be followed by one for orange—an optimistic color of health, sociability, and the fulfillment of potential.

GOOD AND BAD

All colors have both positive and negative associations. Generally, clear and bright shades of a color have a positive, pleasing effect, while its dark, cloudy shades evoke a more negative response.

WHAT THE COLORS OF YOUR CLOTHES SAY ABOUT YOU

If you are going to a job interview, for example, or meeting someone for the first time, study the information below to see how the color of your clothes can help you to project the image you desire.

blue
Sky blue suggests that you have a sincere, sensitive, creative, and trustworthy personality; darker blue suggests that you are decisive, intelligent, and responsible.

orange
You seem extrovert, energetic, adventurous, and full of ideas. You signal that you can be relied upon to take action and get results.

red
You are passionate and brave, a good leader with high standards. In some contexts, red worn by women may carry a sensual or erotic charge.

yellow
You exude confidence and happiness, suggesting that you are intelligent, clear-thinking, and able to cope with challenges. You are resourceful and positive in outlook.

indigo
Indigo or violet projects a compassionate nature. You love knowledge and peace, and find satisfaction in helping others.

pink
You have confidence in yourself and are at peace with your feminine, intuitive side.

brown
Down-to-earth and reliable, you enjoy the good life—food, drink, and conviviality. You can be relied on to avoid flights of fancy.

green
Calm and diplomatic, you are good at finding peaceful solutions. You have an open, observant mind and no fear of change—although you are cautious when necessary.

purple
You seem to be a spiritual and intuitive person who shows great sensitivity.

white
You seek perfection. You carry joy in your heart, and are optimistic about the way forward. You follow your own path and are not dependent on the approval of others.

black
Authoritative, strong-willed, and well organized, you give the impression of inner strength. You are efficient and self-controlled, probably a good leader. Wearing black and gray—the colors of monks and priests—may suggest that you prefer a simple life.

vibrational harmonies

Few of us dress in a single color, choosing instead to team a dominant color with secondary colors whose vibrational energy harmonizes both with our state of mind and with the main color. Sometimes we choose a color designed to boost our sense of wellbeing or project a particular image, but then undermine the effect by mixing it with a disruptive color. Equally, in some color mixes, the secondary color reinforces the effect of the main one to make us feel calmer, more focused, or more impassioned. The effect of your color mix is enhanced when you use a dark shade of one color with a light tint of the other. A rust-red jacket or cardigan offsets a cream shirt or blouse, and suggests that you are adventurous and enthusiastic but also have a balancing strain of perfectionism; your dark gray suit looks elegant when matched with a pale pink blouse or shirt, and projects an impression of competence and self-confidence with a touch of intuition.

COLORS AND COMPLEXION

Keep your natural coloring in mind when choosing clothes.
Greens tend to be a safe bet for everyone.

if you have dark hair and a dark complexion,
your recommended colors are white, bronze or gold, turquoise, dark or pale blue, green.

if you have dark hair and a light complexion,
your colors are black, white, dark blue, turquoise, green.

if you have fair hair and high skin color,
your colors are rose, pink, blue-purple, aquamarine, green.

if you have fair hair and pale skin,
your colors are brown, golden yellow, blue and green, maroon.

if you have red hair,
your colors are dark brown, deep blue, green, orange, terracotta.

A FULL-SPECTRUM OUTFIT

If your spirits and vitality levels are high, you can mix colors as you please. In this state of mind, you will not suffer negative effects from combinations whose vibrational energy might upset you when you are feeling low. For pure enjoyment and self-expression, you could try mixing all the colors of the rainbow in your outfit—but make sure you keep some of them inconspicuous. You might want to wear a red T-shirt with sky-blue jeans and green socks, for example, but confine other strong colors to underwear, jewelry, and accessories.

COMBINING COLORS IN AN OUTFIT

When deciding which colors to combine for a positive effect, consult the color wheel on page 15.

complementary colors
Hues on opposite sides of the wheel go together well; their energies balance and boost one another. Orange and dark blue or yellow and violet, for example, make striking, vibrant contrasts.

bicomplementary colors
Mixing a color with the color alongside the complementary on the color wheel (its bicomplementary) is another good recipe. For example, if you mix orange with blue-green, the outfit will have a positive impact. If you want to replace the violet slacks you wore with your yellow shirt, a blue-violet pair will do as well.

harmonious colors
Neighboring colors frequently combine well. If you mix tones of the same color or of neighboring colors, the contrast will boost the enlivening or calming effect of that range of the spectrum. If you wear slacks in navy blue with a sky blue shirt and a royal-blue tie or brooch, you will be calmed and project an image of creativity tempered by responsibility.

workaday *colors*

For some of us, one of the worst aspects of Monday morning is putting away the bright, expressive clothes of the weekend and clambering back into a work outfit. But we all have plenty of opportunities to express ourselves with color, even in the context of our working lives.

COLOR AT WORK

If you have to wear a uniform at work, you usually won't have to put it on until you clock in, so why not select an outfit in mood-enhancing colors to wear on the way to and from work? Choose your accessories with care—even during the day you will absorb the color vibrations of your underwear or the T-shirt or other clothing you wear under a uniform.

If you feel a strong attraction to particular colors, carry colored cloths or cards with you. You can either display them around your work area or, if there is somewhere where you can relax in private,

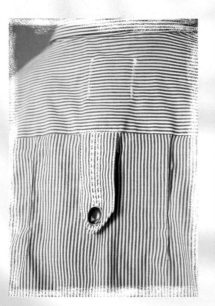

CORPORATE COLORS

Some corporations ask staff to wear uniforms to project an image. What are the subliminal meanings of uniforms worn by staff in courier firms, restaurant chains, or local street-cleaning and garbage-collection teams?

orange
polite and happy, friendly when interacting with the public, lively

blue
reliable, calm in an emergency

green
approachable, cooperative outlook, capable at outdoor work such as tending parks or gardens

brown
helpful, solid and secure, not self-important

red
quick in response, will find solution to problems

yellow
good at understanding and communicating ideas

use them to soothe your spirits or boost your energy levels during your break. If allowed, wear a brooch or ring–or carry a gemstone–in one of your preferred colors.

DRESSING FOR THE JOB

Some colors are particularly well suited to certain occupations, while others should be avoided. For example, if you are a businessperson or banker, black, gray, or dark blue will project authority and reliability. A red tie or other accessory suggests that you are energetic and unstinting in pursuing your clients' goals; accessories in violet or indigo indicate that you are purposeful and capable of inspired thinking.

EMPHASIZING YOUR ROLE

If you are a teacher, a health practitioner, or a complementary healer, wearing blue suggests that you are knowledgeable and dedicated to serving others; light blue suggests a creative capacity for healing. Add orange accents to signal that you have mental energy and independence, or yellow to signal a powerful intellect. If you have to give lectures, be sure to wear bright colors, which will help to make your performance at the lectern eye-catching and memorable. Avoid all-white or all-black outfits.

A lawyer or public servant might wear dark blue or green with a red tie or brooch: the blue suggests dedicated service, and the green an optimistic outlook; red indicates energy and a passionate pursuit of the goal tempered by the more sober blues and greens of the main suit.

Architects, writers, musicians, artists, and designers are free to combine colors to reflect their own preferences and color vibrations. A mixture of bright colors will tend to stimulate creativity while suggesting to potential clients and others that they are fresh-thinking, perhaps unconventional, with an open mind.

If you happen to be pregnant, on maternity leave, a full-time mother, or a kindergarten teacher, wearing green and light blue or pastel shades is soothing for the body and for your young charges.

ACCESSORY COLORS

If you have to wear a dark business suit and sensible shoes to work, you can still express your personality through the colors of the accessories you choose.

red
energetic, has leadership qualities

orange
confident

blue
creative, trustworthy

green
calm, diplomatic

yellow
intellectual, with good reasoning skills

indigo
good team player, easy to work with

violet
understanding, knowledgeable

purple
intuitive

pink
sensitive, confident, flamboyant

time to *unwind*

Many people returning home after a day's work like to change from their business clothes into looser-fitting, perhaps less somber outfits. If you are one of those, pick colors that will help you to relax. If you are feeling stressed after work and want to flop and do nothing at home, choose green, blue, or pastel tints that will encourage you to unwind. Your best bet is to stay natural–you will probably find it easiest to relax if you avoid garments containing artificial colors and fibers.

If you want to unwind totally, choose pajamas or nightgowns in comfortable dark shades of blue and green, perhaps even mauve or purple, rather than bright or busy designs. These will ease your spirits toward restful slumber.

CELEBRATION COLORS

When you are psychologically drained and feeling in need of a lift—say, on a dark winter's evening after trailing home through the rain—energizing colors such as orange or red may help to revitalize you. If you are spending only a short time at home before going out for the evening, change into something bright and cheerful.

Think of the style of clothes you might wear on vacation in a warm place. They will probably be in simple bright colors or complex patterns. Many people find that bringing out these "celebration colors" helps to lift the spirits—not least by recalling the long sunlit days of summer at times when your body is feeling the lack of natural light.

RESISTING FASHION

Whether you are staying in or going out, try to resist being browbeaten by fashion—difficult as that may be when there is nothing but khaki in the stores. You will feel at your best when you are wearing the color scheme that expresses your personality and is attuned to your natural coloring. Don't force yourself into turquoise or silver because it is the color of the moment. If you do, it may make you feel ill at ease because the vibrational energy of the colors you are wearing is at odds with your own energy.

HOW GOOD IS YOUR RELATIONSHIP?

The colors that we choose to wear and surround ourselves with in our own living spaces are eloquent expressions of our personality type. If we are attracted to single colors at particular times—perhaps when we are overworked, depressed, or grieving—this preference reveals a great deal about our state of mind and current aspirations.

Have you thought about whether your natural coloring and color preferences complement those of your partner? Do you find yourself approving of his or her color choices? Or do you wish he or she would take your advice on this matter?

Consider your partner's color choices in clothes, shoes, house furnishings, and decoration—even food. It bodes well for the long-term health of your relationship if your color preferences blend harmoniously.

THE POWER OF GEMS AND CRYSTALS

The tradition of using gemstones and crystals for healing and spiritual strength stretches back at least to the culture of ancient Egypt. Natural stones and crystals embody the power and associations of their color.

Turquoise crystals are highly valued for their protective and healing properties; blue stones promote creativity; yellow stones will help you to think clearly; red ones are energizing and may be useful in stimulating blood flow; green crystals and stones can heal and soothe a troubled spirit; white and sparkling stones can recharge your energy and boost your confidence.

Wear crystals and stones in rings, pendants, bracelets, or brooches. Place them around your home or office to heal your spirits and protect against electromagnetic and spiritual pollution.

the *young* ones

Colors make a strong impression on children from infancy. The play of light and color speaks directly to the spirit and has deep meaning for babies even before they can use words. Toddlers and children will have positive associations for years with a color that they link to a good experience—perhaps the pastel shade of the room where their mother or father lovingly cradled them or the color of their comfort blanket, if they had one. Equally, a color associated with a childhood trauma can make individuals feel uncomfortable or distressed many years afterward.

BABIES

Young babies are constantly adjusting to their surroundings. All is fresh and new, and they are faced with a barrage of sensory stimuli every waking hour. Pastel blues and pinks were the traditional colors for babies' clothes, but the modern fashion in Western society is for bright color combinations and vibrant patterns. There is a view that we should be wary of overstimulation; if you want to protect your baby's sensitivity, you can dress her or him in soft and pale colors with a gentle vibrational energy, such as pale blue, pink, gently earthy greens, cream, and rock grays.

OLDER CHILDREN

Toddlers and older children often favor brighter reds, blacks, blues, and oranges in dynamic patterns. Encourage them to express themselves through color. They will spend plenty of time at kindergarten and elementary school with water-based paints and with crayons in many colors and proudly bring their artwork home. Discuss their color choices with them. Try to get a sense of the colors that speak strongly to them. Use color generously in the home—perhaps by introducing lampshades, rugs, and pillows in the colors of the spectrum in your children's rooms or allowing them to have brightly colored clothes and accessories such as sneakers, hats, and toys.

CHILDHOOD PROBLEMS: COLORFUL SOLUTIONS

Careful use of color can reinforce the effect of medical treatments if your child has physical or behavioral problems.

hyperactive?
He or she may be calmed by wearing blue, green, or yellow, especially in light tones.

skin rash?
Try earthy brown or green in natural fabrics.

can't sleep?
Wear turquoise, blue, or white pajamas and use bed linen in these colors.

asthma?
Wearing blue or white may help to relax muscles and ease symptoms;
do not dress your child in red or black because they often have the opposite effect.

listless and inactive?
Try dressing your child in energizing orange or red.

EARLY TEENS

From around the age of ten into the early teens, children tend to become much more conscious of prevailing fashion and nervous of provoking disapproval at school if they go against what everyone else is wearing. At this age, fashion may largely dictate their color preferences in public, but try to encourage them to keep in mind the colors that speak to them privately and deeply. Help them to keep a place for those colors as long as they retain their significance–perhaps in the choice of pajamas, bathrobe, slippers, or casual "home" clothes.

HEALING COLORS

Color therapists find that children under the age of eight have a particular attraction to and affinity with blue, representing peace, and orange, the color of joy. In those who have the gift of healing, this color affinity lasts into adulthood.

protecting yourself

DOES THE COLOR OF YOUR CLOTHES MAKE YOU UNCOMFORTABLE?

We have all worn clothes that are the right size and cut in a soft natural material but don't feel right. We may be hard pressed to explain precisely why we don't like the shirt or sweater we ignore—but the reason is likely to be that we feel uncomfortable with any color that is subtly discordant with our natural coloring or our color preferences.

We can use the color energy of clothes not only to raise our spirits or give ourselves a lift when we are at a low ebb, but also to protect our bodies and minds against illnesses or negative states of mind.

A red shirt appears red because its fabric absorbs all rays of the spectrum except red. When an individual wears a red shirt, the energizing red vibration passes through the shirt and bathes the body—as well as bouncing off the shirt to make an impression on other people.

When someone wears white, the outfit absorbs none of the vibrations of light, so that the full spectrum of color energy is available to that person; black absorbs all the colors, so a black outfit may provide a soothing "shell" for someone who is feeling in need of protection. If we are attuned to our mental and physical needs, we can choose colors to protect against destructive patterns of thinking and to boost particular body systems.

DON'T WORK AGAINST YOURSELF

When you feel gloomy, picking out a bright color or bright accessory for your business outfit may restore your spirits. But when you are feeling good, avoid wearing colors that work against your mood. If you awaken buzzing with optimism and full of energy, choose bright colors such as orange that reflect your state of mind. If you wear an all-gray or all-black outfit on a day of joy, you may end up feeling subtly discordant.

COLORS AND CHAKRAS

According to the Hindu theory of the chakras (see pages 120–121), each of the body's seven chakras or energy centers is attuned to a color and corresponds to a body system. For example, the throat chakra is attuned to blue and corresponds to the respiratory system—therefore, if you are prone to suffer from panic attacks accompanied by breathing difficulties, wearing soothing blue tones will be beneficial. The solar plexus, just below the navel, is attuned to yellow and corresponds to the digestive and nervous systems—therefore, yellow may help prevent indigestion. For a full list of the chakras and their associated colors and body systems, see page 126.

COLOR COMBINING FOR HEALTH

When choosing colors to boost mental or physical wellbeing, take care which secondary colors you combine with them—some colors will change the effect of the first-choice color. White is generally a safe choice and can be worn with any other color.

if your first-choice color is purple,
team it with blue or white.

if your first-choice color is blue,
a health-promoting partner is white or, sometimes, turquoise.

if your first-choice color is green,
turquoise is a good secondary.

if your first-choice color is magenta, pair it with white;
avoid violet or red.

if your first-choice color is violet,
choose white; avoid blue and magenta.

if your first-choice color is red,
team it with yellow or white.

if your first-choice color is orange,
make the secondary yellow or white; avoid red.

if your first-choice color is yellow,
combine it with white.

seasonal rhythms

We all experience the rhythms of nature—in the hours of light and darkness, in the changing seasons, in our fluctuating physical appetites and energy levels. We also have changing attitudes to, and affinities with, color. In the long bright days of summer we tend to choose lighter colors such as pinks, sky blues, creams, and whites; in the gloomy days of winter we are often drawn to darker shades of warming colors such as reds and oranges. We may find we dress in harmony with the seasons—bright blossom colors in spring, and leafy reds and greens in the fall. Equally, we might choose to go against seasonal effects, dispersing some of the dark of winter by donning the colors of summer or spring. If you keep track of the colors for which you feel a need, you will gain a deeper understanding of your biorhythms.

A COLOR DIARY

Try keeping a record in a small book or folder of the colors that attract you at different times of the week and month, and through the changing seasons. You can collect swathes of material, postcards of paintings or views, paint-sample cards, clippings from magazines, or even photocopies from home-decorating books. If you are feeling

artistic, record your color impressions in wax crayon, pastels, or watercolor. In fall, gather and press some of the wonderfully colored leaves found during a country walk, on a city sidewalk, or in the park.

Your diary will help you to keep track of your color moods and enthusiasms, as well as enabling you to align your color needs retrospectively with changes in physical health or spiritual buoyancy. Looking back, were you drawn to a particular color at a time of illness or stress? When you felt joyful and fully confident of your capacity to rise to challenges, which colors were you in tune with?

Constituting your own personal compendium of colors, the diary will also prove a valuable resource if you are choosing colors for home decoration or for planting in the garden.

WHAT "MISSING" COLORS REVEAL ABOUT YOU

The colors that attract you in clothes and in other parts of your daily life may reflect a lack of the vibrational energy associated with those colors.

blue
If you notice a desire for blue, you are probably low on blue energy, which is associated with peace, decisiveness, and intuition. To escape feelings of stress and distraction, make time to consider your options and do creative work.

red
An attraction to red may indicate lethargy, lack of energy, and frustration with a drab routine. Perhaps you should change your exercise or sleep regime, or alter your diet to boost your vitality.

green
If you long for green, your spirit appears to be crying out for a soothing period of rest; try to take a step back from pressing circumstances in order to recuperate in natural surroundings and gain a fresh perspective.

indigo or violet
A longing for indigo or violet suggests that you are feeling cut off from your higher self. Consider taking a retreat or resuming a form of artistic self-expression—painting or music, for example—that you may have abandoned. Look at the decisions you make every day. You may be very busy—but how many of your activities are necessary? How many could you give up with no loss to yourself or to others? Do you really have to sit in on that meeting? Do you get anything from watching that TV show? Indigo and violet energy will be abundant in your life when you have time to do things slowly, carefully, and with full attention—when you have the peace occasionally to sit in silence and listen to your inner voice.

orange
A desire for orange suggests that you are feeling run down and in need of fresh impetus. Perhaps you have recently weathered a bad illness: you feel gloomy and trapped, and are drawn to the color of joy. Consider your leisure activities—do you have time for recreation?
Try to reorganize your day to make space for yourself. Perhaps you need to look up an old friend who always cheers you up.

yellow
If you miss yellow, linked with happiness, self-confidence, and wisdom, you may feel overwhelmed by challenges and in need either of support or of time to draw upon your own mental resources.

going *natural*

Clothes made from artificial fibers are usually cheaper to buy and easier to wash and handle than equivalent outfits made from natural fabrics. Modern manufacturers have developed an astonishing range of synthetic dyes–producing "convenience clothes" in garish colors and flamboyant patterns. But, as we develop our awareness of color and of our bodies' sensitivities, we frequently discover that we prefer the look and feel of natural fabrics and colorings. Unbleached and undyed cotton, for example, often sets off our natural skin coloring better than a bleached bright-white material. The unbleached cloth comes in a range of subtle light browns and magnolia whites and creams that have a comfortable look. The material also feels softer to the skin–and, unlike bleached cloth, does not release traces of chemicals when washed.

Artificial fabrics do not sit easily on our bodies. Most football jerseys and many running shirts and shorts are made from lightweight, hard-wearing nylon that is very convenient, but also interferes with our skin functions.

When we wear nylon, our skin cannot breathe, and the material generates static electricity that interferes with our bodily vibrations. Cotton shirts and sportswear may be more work to wash and dry, but they are far more comfortable to wear.

NATURAL TEXTURES

Texture is an important aspect of how clothes look. Different natural materials hold color and absorb light in varying ways. Silk has a fine texture and holds rich colors; light playing on silk creates a delicate sheen that suggests the material's luxurious softness. Coarser in texture, wool holds natural dyes very well and can be used for pullovers, coats, and suits in a wonderful range of colors. Cotton is an ideal material for work clothes because it is hard-wearing but also lets the skin breathe.

NATURAL LOOKS

Beauty shines from within—in a bright smile, sparkling eyes, a healthy glow to the skin. We safeguard our natural good looks by taking care of ourselves—making sure our diet contains a balance of minerals and vitamins, drinking plenty of water, getting as much sleep as we need. We do not need makeup to look beautiful, but most of us share the ancient desire to add drama and contrast to our faces with color, and sometimes use makeup for self-expression and fun. Equally, many of us sometimes feel the need to take "emergency action" if we are looking particularly run down or unwell. Just as natural materials harmonize with our physical being better than synthetic fibers, so eye makeup and lipsticks that convincingly mimic the colors of flesh complement our looks better than conspicuously artificial products.

MATERIAL HIERARCHY

Some branches of esoteric theory teach that each human being has four energy bodies.

On the familiar, visible plane we have our physical body. Beyond that we have our life–force, the form of energy identified as *chi* in Chinese schools of thought. At the next level we have our individual soul, and beyond that the higher self or spirit through which in meditation or religious experience we can acquire the sure knowledge that all life is one in God.

Experts associate each of the four most common natural fabrics with one of these energy bodies: wool is attuned to the physical body, linen to the life-force, cotton to the individual soul, and silk to the spirit. A piece of silk dyed purple, indigo, or violet, colors of intuition and the spirit, has an unusual power.

color in your *home*

colorful interiors

We all want the colors we use in our homes to create a memorable impact, but assessing the right colors and color combinations for each part of a living space can be a challenging task. For example, think of the last time you visited an apartment or a house for the first time. What stimulated your initial response? First impressions are crucial. If you devote time and effort to planning the decoration of the front door, the hall, and the rooms leading off it, you will be pleasurably ushered into your home each time you return—and your living space will have a positive effect on visitors.

COLOR HARMONY

If you imagine the colors you combine in one area of your home as voices singing together in a band or choir, you will get a sense of the importance of harmony and of the total effect. To make a pleasant sound, the voices must not only be in tune with one another, but must also blend in terms of volume, timbre, and sound quality. And it helps if they are singing the same song.

Harmony is the overriding consideration. The choir may have voices that are beautifully balanced in terms of timbre and volume, but if they sing in different keys the performance will not be pleasing. Likewise, when decorating your home, you may carefully balance colors for lightness and saturation, but if they do not harmonize, the effect will be jarring.

MAKING GOOD PAIRS

If you are in any doubt about how to combine colors, you can refer to the color wheel (see opposite and page 15) to determine which colors will go well together and which color combinations are likely to be appropriate in different rooms.

For example, you will achieve a bold and striking contrast if you combine complementary colors–those that are directly opposite each another on the color wheel, or those one-third of the way around the wheel from one another. Such a pairing can often be tiring to live with, so, while it might be suitable for a children's playroom, it should probably be avoided in the principal living room.

ASPECTS OF COLOR

The impression we create in our homes depends not only on our choice of color, but also on the color's temperature, saturation, lightness, and "movement."

temperature
Referring to a color's "feel," temperature reflects the contexts in which we find the color in the natural world. For example, orange-red suggests fire and has a warming feel, while blue may make us think of water pools and has a cooling effect.

saturation
The darkness or paleness of a color reflects its saturation. Yellow, for instance, can range from a dark banana hue to the palest lemon wash. Combining a color with white creates a pale "tint"—for example, a pale blue pastel; combining a color with black creates a dark "shade"—such as a brown created by mixing yellow and black.

lightness
The lightness of a color reflects its proximity to white or black. Yellow appears lighter than blue because it is closer to white.

movement
The illusion of a color approaching or retreating from the eye is called movement. Warmer colors such as red appear to move toward the observer, making a room seem smaller, while cooler colors such as light blue seem to move away from the observer, making the most of a room's size.

MAGNETIC AND ELECTRICAL COLORS

Color therapy adds a dimension to our understanding of color by referring to warm hues such as red/orange as magnetic colors and cool ones such as blue and violet as electrical colors. Magnetic colors are linked to the earth and our physical being, while electrical colors are associated with the sky and connect to our spiritual essence.

Blind people—whose lack of sight encourages them to develop an enhanced sensitivity to the vibrations of the electromagnetic spectrum—can often tell magnetic colors from electrical colors by touch alone.

combining *colors*

One of the joys of using color in the home is that you can afford to be adventurous. If you make a mistake and find that the color mixture you have chosen is unsatisfactory, you can easily and relatively inexpensively paint part of the room. But, if you spend plenty of time planning, you are unlikely to go wrong. Don't play safe–the right combination, one that speaks to your soul, will be a source of peace or joy every day for as long as you stay alive to its influence.

DON'T RUSH

Test color combinations before taking the plunge. Buy sample cans of paint and paint small patches of wall. This will give you a good idea of how the colors will look in their setting.

If you don't want to paint onto the wall, you can approximate the effect by painting the samples onto sheets of paper and hanging them in the room, but this will not give you such a clear idea of how the color combination will look on the texture of your wall.

Take your time. See how the colors appear at different times of the day, when the light falls in a particular way. Ideally, you should wait a

---

CHOOSING GUIDE COLORS

Guide colors—those that form the basis of your color scheme—
can be chosen instinctively.

Assemble a selection of paint manufacturers' color cards, magazine or book reproductions, swathes of material, and splashes of sample paint on paper. Try to make sure that your selection represents a wide range and includes all the main colors of the spectrum.

Pin your samples to the wall and sit in front of them for a few minutes. Close your eyes briefly.

Under your breath make the following pledge: "I will find the colors that have meaning for me, that will uplift and guide me."

Open your eyes slightly and view the colors through narrowed lids. One or two colors will connect with you. Pick them at once without analytical thought.

Base a scheme on those colors, trying different shades and tones.

few months to see if your feeling changes as the light shifts from one season to the next.

THE BIG PICTURE

Our perception of a color is altered by the colors we see alongside and around it, so it is wise to consider the look of an entire room rather than just one corner at a time. There may be existing components of a decorative scheme that need to be worked around—a deep-red Afghan rug, say, or a work of art or large film poster that forms the centerpiece of a living-room wall. If you are in the mood for a complete makeover, you may decide to move the rug elsewhere or put away the work of art for a while, but otherwise you will need to make sure that your decorative scheme harmonizes with their colors.

PLAY OF LIGHT

When making decisions about color, consider how the room you are painting will be lit. For example, does it receive warm sunlight or a cooler, northern daylight? If there is very little natural light, you may want to use a mixture of wall-mounted and freestanding light fixtures to provide illumination. You have a wide choice of types of bulb, producing different qualities of light.

You may want to use colored lights in the room or to add color to natural light by means of window hangings made from fabric or stained glass. In some rooms, you may plan to use candlelight most evenings.

you and *yours*

Unless you live alone, most of the rooms in your home will be used by more than one person. When planning to decorate such rooms, you should try to take everyone's color preferences into account, but that doesn't mean settling for a bland compromise—with a little creativity, it is usually possible to come up with a mutually satisfactory color mix.

Try repeating the guide-color exercise (see page 50) with your roommate, partner, or children. It may turn out that your color preferences blend harmoniously with those of other people—but, if not, some negotiation will be necessary.

In theory, there is nothing to stop you from having strikingly different color schemes in different rooms to accommodate the guide colors identified by each individual—a passionate red in your room, say, with pink and purple in your daughter's bedroom.

But you also need to consider the effect of moving from one room to the next and, where it applies, the effect of being able to see into one

(see page 50)

THE RIGHT COLORS FOR THE ROOM

When planning a color scheme, ask yourself the following questions.

How big is the room?

Do I need to make it look bigger? (If so, choose cool rather than warm colors.)

What is the room used for?

Do I want a restful, zesty or illuminating atmosphere?

If people share the room, can I combine their color preferences in a scheme that pleases everyone?

ADDING COLOR

Apart from paint and wallpaper, there are many ways to add color to a room. Some elements have the advantage of being easily removable, allowing you to vary the look of the room season by season or simply when you desire a change.

light
colored window glass, hanging crystals, colored bulbs or candles, lightbox or projector

walls
hanging fabrics, posters, paintings, wall-mounted candle-holders or light fixtures, your own artwork, hand-painted tiles

floors
rugs, wall-to-wall carpets, other floor coverings such as linoleum or seagrass, or hand-painted tiles

objects
painted furniture, vases, bowls and china pieces, flowers, colored throws over furniture, cushions, curtains, tablecloths, a movable wooden screen with mounted colored paper

room from another. If you can see into the kitchen from the family room, say, you need to make sure the color schemes of the two rooms do not clash. Even when you cannot see from one room to the next, you will probably want to avoid a jolting feeling when you move from one color scheme to a second.

COLOR IDEAS

If you are stumped for ideas, look around you. Color inspiration is on every side. In spring, the delicate pink and white blossoms on the trees contrast with the deep maroon of a parked car; at the end of the street you glimpse a rainbow. In summer, you see a yellow sweep of wheatfield against the blue sky. In fall you take pleasure in the hues of root vegetables or the delicate complexity of reds and rusty browns in fallen leaves. Winter surprises you with a red burst of berries against evergreen or a splash of yellow sunlight suspended in misty air. Visit an art gallery or look at some home decorating books and magazines for other ideas. Recall your travels—think of the bright colors used in India, Mexico, South Africa. Sometimes you may want to plan a whole color scheme around a treasured possession such as an antique vase or an inherited set of cups and saucers.

colors for *energy* and *stimulation*

For an environment that will stimulate and energize you, choose reds, oranges, and rich yellows. Red is the color of blood, of types of earth and flowers, of rich dark wine. It has the power to boost the circulation and quicken the pulse. It is also the color of warning lights, stop signs and fire engines—it can grab your attention and trigger action.

COLORS OF NATURE

Natural materials are an effective complement to bright energizing colors. Try offsetting a red or orange wall or alcove with a sofa covered in a throw of unbleached beige-to-cream cotton or contrasting deep yellow walls with the natural gray-green of collected rocks.

Pale wood flooring is effective in offsetting many hot color schemes, not least those dominated by rich red walls or rugs. Conversely, warm, energetic colors make a delightful background if you want to display a treasured object such as a stone carving or a neutrally colored statue.

Red

Red stimulates conversation and debate, and makes people feel "alive." For this reason, red is a favorite among designers in schemes for fashionable bars. Red also encourages activity—so it is perfect for areas where people must be kept moving, such as hotel lobbies. In the home, red can be an excellent color for small hallways or corridors—areas where people may be energized by the color as they pass through. Equally, red is recommended for powder rooms or other small rooms visited in passing. Another benefit of rich reds is that they have the effect of making a room seem warmer, so they can be a good decorative choice for cold rooms tucked away at the back of a house.

Yellow

Radiant full yellows are suggestive of sunlight, and bring an optimistic and fresh feel to a room. Yellow is also associated with mental activity, with analytical thought and the activities of the ego. It makes a good color for a wall in a study or in an area where children do homework.

Yellow is also suitable for rooms used in the morning, such as kitchens or breakfast rooms. Red and yellow together create a welcoming glow, and are therefore an effective combination in a well-lit hallway.

Orange

Orange combines red and yellow–it can be seen as a balancing color that mixes the earthy passion of red with the mental force of yellow. Glowing orange, the color of flames–whether in its earthy, autumnal shades such as rust and terracotta or in its lighter pure orange or peach tints–can boost people's enthusiasm and give them a sense of get-up-and-go. Orange is the color of the sacral chakra (see page 121), which is associated with part of the digestive system, and it therefore tends to stimulate appetite. Orange is often used in restaurants and, if carefully balanced with complementary colors, may be a good choice for a dining area in the home.

Orange also stimulates movement, so it would be a good choice for an exercise room. If you are holding a party that involves dancing, add orange to your color scheme–in the form of colored bulbs, a bright throw over furniture, or an orange rug.

We can have too much red, yellow, or orange. Warm colors in abundance can overstimulate the nervous system–leading to feelings of uneasiness or even anger and aggression. A meeting held in a room decorated with large areas of red or orange may degenerate into disagreement and conflict, whereas one in a cool blue or dark green space is more likely to reach a productive conclusion. If you decorate your bedroom in yellow, a color of clear-thinking and mental activity, you may find yourself stimulated at a time when you need to rest.

Moreover, like other warm colors, reds and oranges tend to move toward the viewer, so will make a room seem smaller. This might not be a problem in a corridor or bathroom, say, where you may not be concerned if the space appears small, but large areas of red or orange are generally inadvisable in a small living room. You can reduce this effect by introducing a counterbalancing color on the ceiling and on the floor–in the form of carpet, painted boards, or rugs. If one or more walls are painted in rich, energizing colors, a pale-colored floor and ceiling provide light relief.

ROOM FOR REDS

If you want to use larger areas of energetic red, vibrant yellow, or intense orange in a decorative scheme, pick your room with care. For example, such use of color is often inappropriate in a bedroom, although some tones of red can create a sensuous atmosphere

---

A PLACE TO CONCENTRATE

The capacity of yellow to stimulate thoughts, banish drowsiness, and foster attentiveness makes it an ideal color for a home study. If your work is creative, try introducing violet, the color of intuition, to balance the power of yellow. A kitchen painted yellow is a welcoming haven for a family, helping everyone to gather their wits in the morning, and also provides a good spot for homework.

MAGNETIC MIXES

If you are using large areas of the warming magnetic colors, look for colors to complement them and offset their energy.

red
complemented by lavender, turquoise, blue and gold.

yellow
complemented by violet, lavender, blue and green.

orange
complemented by indigo, blue and gray.

(see page 60). Likewise, in a bathroom a soothing marine or green color scheme is more conducive to relaxation.

Energizing colors can be effective in a hallway, cloakroom, or powder room, depending on the light available and how dark the paints are. They should be used with care in small living rooms, but reds and oranges can be effective as accent colors.

Welcoming butter yellows are perhaps better than fiery reds in kitchens, where you are unlikely to want to add to the heat, but rich reds and oranges are desirable and well-established choices for dining zones. Yellows are ideal for studies or other areas where mental work takes place; brighter shades of red might be too stimulating, but warm terracotta and rust colors may have the right degree of energizing lift.

When working with these colors, it is important not to overdo it. Large sweeps of red and orange are probably best avoided if you have high blood pressure or a heart condition because the colors, particularly red, are known to stimulate blood circulation. A shade of pink, in which the energizing red has been toned down by white, would provide a safer level of stimulation.

COLOR ACCENTS

Stimulating colors are often best used in small areas as accents. A light shade of a complementary color applied in large blocks will provide a background against which a dark red or russet orange, for example, can lift a room.

The greater the contrast between accent and background color, the smaller the area of accent should be.

Use shades of blue and gray to complement orange and turquoise, or a darker green to complement red.

Paint an alcove or one part of a wall in an energizing color and the rest in a complementary color.

Try painting the wall behind a bookshelf a warm red or the inside of a cupboard scarlet.

Hang red or orange drapes in a window so that daylight is colored and further energized as it enters the room.

Add contrasts in the form of furniture, vases, bowls, pillows, or fresh fruit.

colors for *romance*

The color pink evokes romantic love, flower-scented arbors, and intimate spaces where we can take refuge from the cares of the world. It is a soothing hue associated by color theorists with compassion and the gentle treatment of self. In the making of pink, white tones down the energy and stimulation represented by red.

PEACEFULNESS AND LOVE OF HOME

A pink-themed room may help to defuse conflict, encouraging a relaxed and loving approach, while in a red room, anger may be more common. But pink does not foster weakness or loss of self-respect; on the contrary, it is linked with a well-developed sense of justice, of right and wrong. Although pink suggests a person who shows unconditional love, it does not imply that such a person is weak. Pink contains the strength and life and earthiness of red.

Color theorists say that rose-pink tones are an ideal choice for people who revel in home life, consolidating the love of home as a place of nurturing and growth. Children often favor pink instinctively; graduated pinks may be a good color scheme for those who wish to express their romantic personality through love of partner and family. Peach pink, which combines pink and orange, is warmer and more physical in its associations, while mauve pink, a mixture of blue and pink, is cooler and more spiritual.

Creamy white, the color of lilies and white roses, conjures images of a summer room where gauzy curtains flutter in the breeze. Try using several tones of unbleached, creamy white offset by reddish pink, purple, red-mauve, or magenta.

THE RIGHT LIGHT

Appropriate lighting is a crucial part of achieving a romantic effect. Candlelight, which like sunlight contains the full wealth of spectrum colors, casts a delicate glow on walls. Candelabra on a table create an intimate atmosphere for dinner. A room with many candles, perhaps in reds and greens, has a delicate, magical quality and makes a guest feel warmly welcomed.

Low lighting with red or pink-tinged bulbs contributes to an intimate atmosphere even in a functionally decorated room. Using colored bulbs and a few cushions, you can create an enticing pink-to-magenta ambience, say, in a white room that might appear harsh or utilitarian in daylight—ideal for a "chillout room" at a party.

A FEMININE COLOR?

Pink is often identified as feminine in contrast to the more masculine vibrancy of red. Pink remains a traditional choice for nurseries and baby girls' clothes, which may explain its resonance as a color of safety and unconditional love.

Whether you are male or female, choosing pink tends to indicate that you take pleasure in and derive confidence from your feminine side. You are not afraid to be intuitive or make yourself vulnerable by opening your heart and expressing tenderness.

Red, pink, or violet translucent window hangings make good use of daylight, introducing a romantic coloring into a space. A room lit in this way is a haven, filling people with a gentle dose of color energy and helping them to set their busy minds at rest. Hanging colored-glass beads or standing colored-glass vases on the windowsill creates a few moments of immediate beauty when the sun shines, touching us with an intense experience of the here and now.

MODERN PINKS

To some modern tastes, traditional pinks may seem washed-out or wishy-washy, but pink comes in many more lively tones. Shocking magenta pink and lighter sugar pink have an insistence and vibrancy that can make them tiring to live with, but used with care they produce a burst of joy, a splash of heartening pleasure. Magenta, which combines red and violet, has an elevating spiritual aspect when used

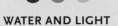

WATER AND LIGHT

The play of light on water is a source of fascination and delight. Try floating votive candles in a large bowl of water or standing colored candles behind a large goldfish bowl so they are visible through the water.

with restraint. But some of us seek an ambience that ignores restraint and indulges excess–such as in a highly romantic and contemporary combination of pink, deep reds, and touches of orange.

SENSUOUS REDS

Deep red, the color of the heart and of desire, can arouse passion; a red wall or red accents in a more gentle color scheme quicken the emotions and move ardent feeling to expression.

Color theorists advise against having red in a bedroom because it is said to be too stimulating for a place of repose. But color tastes are highly individual—and red's associations with sensuous pleasure

encourage some people to use it in the bedroom, where it can be expected to conjure feelings of intimacy and physical abandon.

Avoid bright reds; if a room is small, be wary of emphasizing its limited dimensions. Skillful placement of mirrors and use of natural and electric light can counter a shrinking effect.

RED AND MAGENTA

Red and magenta speak to us at opposite ends of our physical continuum. Red is the color associated with the base chakra at the bottom of the spine, while magenta flows to the crown chakra at the top of the head (see page 121). Red links us to our environment, energizing and warming our bodies; magenta lifts us from the physical to the spiritual, feeding our soul.

THE ROMANCE OF THE EXOTIC

The deep tones of Indian terracotta, the lift of bright Mexican blue, and the warm sandy ocher of northern Africa suggest the excitement of the unfamiliar. These colors derive from natural pigments used largely undiluted under fierce local sunlight. In northern areas, where light is more diffused, we may want to tone down their brightness, but color schemes based on these evocative colors have an instant exotic appeal.

A bedroom with terracotta walls and rich red bed coverings offers a safe retreat, evoking the idea of a cozy place of recuperation such as a burrow or cave. Potted houseplants, a few mantelpiece ornaments, and the color range of books on a bookcase add contrast.

Another way to introduce an exotic touch into your home is to buy imported patterned tiles and set them in the floor in front of your fireplace or put them in your bathroom or kitchen. You can also paint your own tiles in evocative patterns using special ceramic paints.

EFFECTS OF COLORED LIGHT

Color therapists warn against using green-tinted light in the home, arguing that it does not help us to thrive. But other tinted lights can have positive effects.

rosy pink light
is intimate and seductive.

red light
is stimulating and energizing (for example, the effect of daylight passing through a red gauze hanging).

blue light
is very soothing.

violet light
promotes peace, gentleness.

golden yellow light
provides an uplift, bringing happiness.

colors for *soothing* and *relaxation*

Green promotes healing and harmony. Except for its very yellow lime shades, green is restful on the eye; combining yellow and blue, it is a color of balance, associated with the heart chakra (see page 121) and feelings of self-acceptance and security.

At times of loss, or when we are feeling bruised following a failed love affair or suffering a sense of rejection in the world of work, a green room or a green area in a room offers natural regeneration and a saving, bolstering influence. Green provides balance, but also needs to be balanced itself. Too much green can be stultifying—you can be soothed too much, and end up slipping into lethargy and indolence.

SINGING THE BLUES

Deep blue is a calming color for a bedroom ceiling. Add accents in bright colors—in a child's room, for example, you could paint yellow, white, or orange stars on the ceiling to emulate the heavens. Daytime sky or water blues on the walls complement this color combination, and graduating the movement from dark blue to lighter blues—by adding increasing amounts of white to the ceiling blue—makes an entrancing effect at the edge of the ceiling and down the walls.

Blue is a color of rest, making it an excellent stress-buster after a hard day's work. In addition to soothing the mind, it encourages muscular relaxation and settled breathing. Color therapists recommend blue for the prevention of nightmares and the treatment of insomnia. A headache brought on by overwork or worry and tension will gradually ease in a predominantly blue room. Indeed, the majority of people—just over 50 percent—name blue as their favorite color, evidently cherishing its restful, nurturing qualities.

Blue-greens have a cooling effect—delightful in a well-lit space or a hot climate, but perhaps inadvisable in a cold, north-facing room. Turquoise and other marine blues, with their hint of sea-pools, summon a profound calm. They are both relaxing and lively, gentle but full of impact.

Lighter blues, greens, and tints of turquoise retreat from the eye, making a small room appear bigger. They encourage expansive thought, perhaps encouraging self-sufficiency—for this reason, they may need spicing up with warm magnetic colors.

Marine blues open up space, making them an ideal choice for a very small room such as a powder room or shower room.

YELLOW AND BLUE

Yellow and blue make a soothing combination that works well in any room. From the palest of yellow and sky blue to the deepest buttery orange-yellow and dark blue, this restful, healing color scheme lifts the spirits.

Yellow walls in a kitchen make the most of available light and blend harmoniously with the warmth of a table, floor covering, or countertop in natural wood, while blue accents add interest. The colors soothe frazzled nerves when the oven is pumping out heat and the baby screaming is for attention. Stainless-steel equipment and appliances satisfactorily complement blue walls.

A yellow and blue combination in a bathroom suggests a sun-drenched seascape and will help to ease you into a calm, meditative frame of mind for a healing soak in a hot bath.

GROUNDING COLORS

Deep and tan browns, natural greens, wood tones, brick, terracotta, stone, and unbleached white-cream all bolster the feeling of belonging to the earth. Surrounding yourself with these colors should give you a strong sense of being in your natural environment.

Brown suggests simplicity, self-control, and commitment. It is the color of the robes traditionally worn by Catholic monks of the Franciscan order. An easy and satisfying way to introduce brown into your home is to use natural wood. Floors, ceilings, wall panels, door frames, chairs, tables, chests of drawers, bookcases, and picture frames can all be marshaled to add grainy texture and shades of earthy brown to your décor.

Gray, another color often adopted for monastic habits, is a soothing, balancing agent—both with light, bright hues such as orange and with darker browns. The natural gray of pebbles and stones often contains veins and spots of other colors.

When working with grays and browns, it is advisable to stick to natural materials—wood, wool, leather, stone—since these colors can seem rather heavy when used as pigments in paint.

DARK BLUE CALM

Dark blue can be used to introduce an oasis of calm in a place where patience may run short or tempers fray. Perhaps you have a home office and occasionally host work meetings there—a blue area of wall, a blue partition, or a predominantly blue work of art will provide an injection of cool. Equally, a dark blue stove, cupboard, or piece of stained glass might be enough to soothe a stressed cook in the kitchen.

SOOTHING LIGHT

The colors in light have a deeper and more penetrating effect than pigments used in paint. Light makes an impact unconsciously, directly on the body cells, whereas paint colors affect only the conscious mind. Colored lights can be powerfully soothing in milder color schemes.

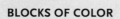

BLOCKS OF COLOR

Painted effects on walls add interest to a room. Blocks of contrasting color derived from the blue-green palette and given a gentle, washed appearance bring easy, soothing movement. But be careful with bold patterns in brighter colors, stripes, and horizontal lines. They tend to have a more insistent, energizing effect than would be desirable in a room intended for relaxation.

There is a tendency for soothing color schemes in brown and cream or brown and stone to appear a little impersonal, to suggest a neutral elegance of the kind sometimes adopted in rented apartments or hotels. In a home setting, browns may need to be lifted with brick-orange or light creams to make a pleasing combination. Add a dash of color with flowers, peacock feathers, ceramics, cotton or woolen throws, or a vibrant rug.

Terracotta brings warm, earthy tones to a soothing color scheme, providing a rosy glow that offers a gentle lift of red. Mixed from natural pigments, it has a traditional feel but also a touch of the exotic, evoking as it does rich Indian and other oriental decorative schemes (see page 61). Combining terracotta with yellows and rich gold generates a welcoming, comfortable atmosphere; terracotta is a wonderful choice for north-facing rooms that receive a whitish light, since it introduces a cozy pink warmth.

PASTEL APPROACHES

Muted pastel tones create a light, gentle atmosphere evocative of a beach cottage or a garden summerhouse. Soft blues, pinks, mauves, turquoises, and greens, teamed with white, make the most of the light in even the gloomiest or chilliest of rooms. A touch of gray introduces a note of distinction if you want to prevent a color scheme from becoming too pretty.

Pastel checks in blue and white are a traditional favorite for chairs and cushions in a predominantly white room. Pink and white and floral patterns add gentle warmth. You may be drawn to the cottage look and feel it is a well-tried and appropriate way to use these colors. A more modern, urban angle would be to marshal pastels in single-color blocks painted on white or cream walls. This provides a pleasing and distinctive, but still gentle, double act. Pastels and white are a relaxing combination because they do not set up a strong contrast, making them restful to look at.

According to the Chinese science of feng shui, pastel tints significantly affect our wellbeing. Pale blue and minty green are linked with relaxation, pink with youthfulness and play, lavender with the joy of company, and magnolia with peace.

WHITE

A color scheme based on white offers a fresh environment suggestive of wide expanses of empty air or countryside blanketed in snow. Some people find white soothing because it delivers a sense of blankness and emptiness–they rejoice in feeling free and in having the space to be themselves. In color theory, white is associated with innocence, neutrality, cleanliness, and wisdom. If you are confused and in need of time to sort out your thoughts, you may benefit from living in a white environment. White also has undeniable elegance and can be pleasingly complemented by glass furniture and bright fixtures. But white is also the color of solitude–use too much white and you risk making yourself feel isolated. There are many whites to choose from, ranging from shades of creamy-yellow to those of gray or orange-pink; avoid blue-undertone whites, which can be extremely chilly.

BLACK

When combined with the right color accents, black can be a powerful decorative hue. In color theory, black is the color of knowledge and humble thinking. But it is also associated with being negative, and black interiors can seem depressing. The Chinese say that black in the home is lucky and tend to combine it with bright shades of red.

Black certainly needs to be handled sensitively, supported with warm-toned neutral colors and energized with red or bright green. Choose the surface treatment with care–black gloss produces a shiny finish that brightens the overall effect by reflecting light. Consider coating part of a wall or the inside of a bathroom door in blackboard paint and providing chalk for guests and family members to write reminder notes, schedules, and graffiti.

SILVER AND GOLD

Subtle touches of silver and gold will add elegance and opulence to a soothing color scheme. Gold, traditionally a color of wisdom and plenty, combines particularly well with warm reds and oranges, whereas silver, which projects serenity and knowingness, offsets cool blues and greens.

AMBIVALENT EGGPLANT

Eggplant combines the earthy comfort of brown with the luxury of purple. Depending on the proportion of these colors in the mix, and the ambient lighting, eggplant can be restful or slightly more energetic. Both tones sit nicely with a sophisticated look—they go well with fireplaces, candlesticks, picture- and mirror-frames, and ornaments in silver and gold, and their richness complements velvet curtains or throws. Cream or white walls offset the deep, relaxing tones of aubergine pillows or upholstery.

colors for *meditation*

A meditative color scheme should help us to turn off our mental clock. Energizing colors such as red appear to make us more aware of time and our physical being, while blue, green, indigo, violet, and magenta lift us away from the cycles of time toward the spiritual plane.

Violet and magenta are usually best limited to accents–with violet, perhaps in an earthy-yellow color scheme, and with magenta in a largely blue combination. Add small amounts of these uplifting colors through cushions, rugs, a large vase, a floral display, the frame of a mirror, or paint around a fireplace or small bookcase.

GREEN AND BLUE

Colors such as green and blue, which are closely associated with the natural world, give us the strength to remain grounded in and embraced by the physical realm as we move closer toward a state of greater spiritual calm. Green is regarded as a color of compassion. In its darker tones, it attracts us into a spiritual oasis, a place of understanding and generosity. Blue gently stimulates creativity, encouraging imaginative thought: once we feel relaxed and grounded with blue, we can apply our minds with detachment to the problems confronting us. Blue relieves anxiety and builds self-confidence; it suggests the infinity of space, lifting us from the dense physical world toward violet and magenta and the weightless realm of the spirit.

INDIGO AND VIOLET

Indigo is associated with the brow or third eye chakra (see page 121), situated between and just above the two eyes. Deep indigo evokes the wide expanses of the midnight heavens and the fathoms of sea beneath. It is linked to the freedom and release of non-logical thinking–the deep wisdom of a truth grasped by intuition. Indigo mixes well with pink and orange, and color theory teaches that these combinations can help to free us from fear.

Violet, which adds the energy of red to blue, is the color of the crown chakra at the top of the head and is believed to promote spirituality while bolstering self-respect and dignity. The color is calming and gently uplifting; it soothes the soul, but also awakens higher mental processes, encouraging us to take time out to relax, but also to use the time well. A violet wall or violet accents in a room will lift the spirits of somebody sitting in the room, perhaps prompting that person to step back from the daily routine and reconnect to the inner self.

Violet, like purple, combines feelings of luxury and inspirational mystery—evoking imperial purple or the spiritual elevation of bishops and archbishops. Blue shades of the color, on the cool side of violet, appear to recede; an area of soothing blue-violet may ease the anxieties of people who suffer from claustrophobia.

MAGENTA

In color theory, magenta, the red-violet hue associated with the crown chakra (see page 121), is linked with choice and the processes of spiritual transformation. Magenta has the power to encourage change, the letting go of habits and fears, the movement into freedom. It summons the perfection we may touch or seek in meditation and other religious activity. Magenta combines wisdom gleaned from experience with spiritual aspiration.

GREEN CONTRASTS

A small splash of magenta makes an enlivening contrast with emerald green. Another spiritual color, violet, also works to draw out green and stimulate higher thinking processes.

A SPACE FOR REFLECTION

When we meditate or think reflectively, we are seeking to turn away from the stream of sensory input and calm the ceaseless chatter of our thoughts. A space for meditation or quiet reflection needs to be soothing on the eye, its colors combining to encourage a settled concentration on the inner self. Predominantly cool colors in a room are good if you want to avoid too much physical stimulation. But accents and small areas of warm color are necessary to prevent the space from appearing cold and uninvolving—we often need a lift to help us to move on from one stage to the next.

GOLDEN GLOW

Warm colors such as orange and red have strong religious associations, making them appropriate for a meditative scheme.

Religious ecstasy is often depicted as the touch of orange–red heavenly flames.

As a color of joy, and of some Buddhist monks' robes, orange has a spiritual dimension; in some contexts it is linked with the physical appetites of hunger and, through the sacral chakra, the libido—but it can also be spiritually uplifting

Orange is known to promote feelings of acceptance, which are helpful for the peace and detachment that aids meditation and reflective, intuitive thought.

The glow of golden light is associated with revelation in religious art, where it is often the color of saintly haloes or bursts of heavenly brightness.

While too much yellow boosts intellectual activity and stimulates the ego, rich yellow counterbalanced by a cool green–gray or light blue adds warmth and expansiveness to the quiet of a meditative color scheme.

THE JOY OF NEW LIFE

Relaxing sky blue or white, the color of wisdom, can contain the same lift and challenge as lime, the most vibrant tone of green, which is traditionally associated with the joy of new life in spring.

ACHIEVING DEEP CALM

It is easy to become trapped in an unproductive cycle of thought, replaying in the mind past insults or triumphs in a way that works against our better judgment and keeps us in thrall to the past. Watching the play of natural light on a sky-blue or violet wall can help to calm such niggling thoughts and anxieties. Cool tones such as peacock blue have a deep and expansive feel; they appear infinitely deep as they attract attention, yet they also encourage us to forget our physical being and shift our focus inward.

Pastel blues warmed by creamy yellows and energized by fern green make a gentle combination. Deep blues and indigo are said to be the best colors for meditation; a powerful if very individual approach might be to combine them with violet and purple-mauves, perhaps adding energy with touches of rich red. This would be a rather dark scheme, but would work for a retreat room given plenty of natural light and the added warmth of electric lamps.

By contrast, light pistachio and other yellow-greens are cool and elegant, with a certain finesse; natural wood flooring or furniture adds warming orange contrasts, while darker green, perhaps in a sofa covering or set of curtains, brings depth and definition.

Generally, simplicity is the key for a meditative effect. A monochrome color scheme–several tones of the same color–may work well here. A scheme incorporating several shades of blue from palest sky blue to the deep blues of indigo would provide the right level of variety. Some contrasts in warmer, buttery orange yellows would add lift. Avoid patterns that may work against the dreamy quality that supports reflection and retreat.

color in your *garden*

your style of *garden*

What do you long for in a garden? A burst of color to refresh or calm you, a green and shady spot in which to unwind, a fertile vegetable patch, a heady sweep of floral fragrance to carry you away in memory or fantasy and help you to forget your cares?

In your garden you are touched by the restorative power of nature–simply by being in full-spectrum natural light, by experiencing the soothing cycles of the days and seasons, by receiving the natural color healing of flowers and foliage. Moreover, nature's healing benefits reach out to you in any type of garden, whether you have an expansive lawn with well-established trees, a small neat square of green, a patio behind a row house, or a roof garden outside an upper-story flat.

When I moved from an apartment to a row house with a tiny patio garden, I was struck by the soothing power of the garden despite its small size–I felt a great benefit merely from being able to sit outside beneath the sky, to inhale the fragrance of the honeysuckle that a previous householder had planted, and on a summer's evening to watch the shift of colors in the heavens and the effects of evening light on the flowers and bushes.

If you live in a town or city and your plot is small or hemmed in by other houses, you can still have the deep satisfaction of planning your garden for year-round color and of seeing your hard work in planting and pruning rewarded–say, by a glorious display of pure white, deep red, and glorious yellow against calming green foliage.

But the kind of garden you have to start with determines the strategy for achieving the effects you want. While you will be searching for potted plants, climbers, and trees when planning a patio or roof terrace, you may want to consider planting large banks of flowers or buying in mature trees for a country garden. You also need to consider the prevailing conditions. Does your garden receive evening or morning sunlight? Is the soil well drained? Is it a windy spot? Do frosts come often?

WHAT KIND OF GARDEN DO YOU WANT?

The first step to achieving a therapeutically colorful garden is to decide your priorities. Identify the most appealing garden style and features from this list.

a wild garden
wild grasses and flowers

a kitchen garden
vegetable plot and herb garden

a combination of vegetable patch and lawn;
you may want a hedge or fence to divide up the garden

a place to look out at from inside the house;
as is often the case with small urban gardens, your main concern may be to have a pleasing vista from your dining table

a pond with frogs and fish;
a fountain or other water feature

a place for children to play;
you will want, if possible, to keep delicate flowers and bushes away from areas in which ball games may be played

a place for pet animals

a naturalized garden,
one in harmony with the environment; if you live near the sea, say, find room for driftwood and other found objects

a rock garden

a place to sit at your ease
for instance, in a recliner on the lawn

a place to dine
on a paved area

TIPS FOR A SMALL GARDEN

With careful planning, you can achieve a wonderful variety even in a small city garden or roof terrace.

red, yellow, and lilac
Plant colorful combinations such as tulips, hyacinths, and crocuses in earthenware pots or stone troughs and store in corners, then bring into full view when ready to flower.

white flowers
Grow climbers such as honeysuckle or winter-flowering jasmine on a patio wall or small garden fence or on the back wall of your house.

violet, red, and yellow
Put up a wall basket or hanging basket of petunias, marigolds, geraniums, and trailing lobelia on the wall above a roof terrace.

green flavor
Grow herbs such as mint, chives, or oregano in a windowbox.

red dash
Try raising cherry tomatoes in a windowbox or sunny patio corner. You could fashion an inexpensive greenhouse lean-to if you have space.

garden *color* design

Each garden color has its own spiritual quality and healing energy. Gardeners usually seek to create color contrasts and harmonies, but you may want to plant a corner or windowbox in a single hue in order to benefit from a sizable dose of that color's energy.

COLOR CHOICES

Reds introduce vibrancy and visual drama to any garden. Large areas of red tend to dominate or overwhelm, but they can be balanced by green foliage. A dash of red is a fortunate addition to a garden in winter—on a cold day, red gladdens the spirit and quickens the heart.

Blues suggest peace, the calm of an empty sky or a wide stretch of water. In plants, they range from gentle pastel sky-blues to deep purple-blues; an area of blue in your garden or on your roof terrace will provide an oasis of healing calm.

Pinks soothe anxieties. A few minutes spent contemplating the pink blossom on a cherry tree or a windowbox of pink blooms will immerse you in this gentle color vibration, which draws out an accepting and loving attitude. If you are tense or irritable, pinks will help you be kinder to yourself and others.

Lavender, indigo, and lilac colors elevate the spirit, inspiring you to free yourself from damaging habits that keep you in thrall and to seek the guidance of your higher self. If you meditate in a room with a garden view, plant indigo colors where you can gaze on them from your meditation corner. Indigos and violet-mauves will—like pinks—help you to cope with and overcome tension and anxiety.

An array of white flowers against a bank of green leaves provides a cooling, calming touch of purity, a respite from a busy, noisy life. They suggest the serenity of the moon; some release a heady scent that emphasizes this

GARDEN SYMBOLS

In the Chinese tradition, red flowers signify happiness, business achievement and success in a new venture, and a garden with vibrant green leaves and deeply colored flowers ushers in prosperity and joy, but a neglected and dried-out flowerbed is a portent of unhappiness and meagre times.

otherworldly quality. Make yourself a white-flowered garden corner for a summer evening retreat, a place where you can recharge your batteries and find tranquility of spirit.

Yellows are associated with spring, when we look for the tones of daffodils and primroses to signal the end of winter and a new start. These gentler yellows combine very well with silver or white flowers. Richer golden yellows are generally best marshaled in small areas of the garden, since they can overwhelm other colors. A view of yellow flowers from your study or sitting room boosts vitality and fosters alertness.

Green soothes bruised emotions and aids relaxation. People recuperating from a setback or illness find gentle healing in a day spent pottering in the garden. The many shades of green—an expanse of green lawn, an undulating wall of leaves, a bank of foliage behind flowers—provide intriguing single-color contrasts for the eye. Green complements any other colors you choose for your palette, bringing structure and balance to the garden scheme.

Orange flowers can lift your levels of activity and your mood, and are therefore recommended for anyone suffering from lethargy or depression. They bring a warm blaze of brightness and color energy to a chilly or gloomy garden.

THE SINGLE-COLOR GARDEN

If you plant your entire garden in one predominant color, you will need to make the most of varieties of shape, tone and texture. Add highlights of other colors to create visual movement and depth.

A city garden planted predominantly in green creates a deeply peaceful retreat, summoning the atmosphere of a country idyll and suggesting the depths of reflective thought stimulated by the harmonizing energy of green.

A white-themed garden—planted with silver, gray, and white against a background of deep green—creates a soothing and elevating atmosphere.

Frequently, a garden's single-color effect works best when it comes as a surprise or is revealed suddenly—for instance, if a bank of white or red flowers is hidden around a corner in your garden or shielded from general view by a bank of foliage, a tree, or a garden building. Such an arrangement offers no distant view; each time you come upon the group of plants, you are forced to take them all in at once.

combining garden *colors*

◗ ◗ ◗

SIMPLE EFFECTS?

Sometimes "less is more" in creating effective color combinations. A flowerbed with just two differently colored plant varieties will make a more marked contrast than one with several varieties in shades of the same two colors.

But, if you want depth and more complex effects, then a mixture of many plant varieties will provide an enticing view, a vista of flowers that draws in the eye.

Very few gardeners want more than an isolated burst of single-color effects. For most of us, the art lies in mixing colors in ways that create intriguing contrasts and a pleasing overall effect. When devising a color palette, we consider shades and tints of colors, different textures and shapes, color in foliage, berries, fruits, grasses, garden furniture, walls and light effects as well as in flowers.

Like an artist at an easel, we think of the whole picture–for the effect of colors may vary when they are placed side by side. Plot your color combinations in a pot or tub, within a particular flowerbed, and across the entire garden.

PLANNING CONTRASTS WITH THE COLOR WHEEL

Select adjacent hues from the color wheel (see right and page 15) to build harmonies of color. Alternatively, use different tints and shades of a single color. Pinks, violets, and lilacs make a harmonious combination.

Use complementary colors to make striking contrasts, in which the two colors stand out from one another and emphasize their difference. Poppies and other deeply red flowers look very strong against green, while orange blooms trumpet their color energy against a bed of blues.

THE WIDER ENVIRONMENT

When choosing plant varieties and colors, bear in mind your garden's wider setting. Does it overlook a sweep of countryside or border farm fields? Is it near the ocean? Is it a highly enclosed urban plot? Do you have a roof terrace from which you are mainly aware of the sky?

In a country garden, consider using cultivars of local wild flowers, since they will provide a delightful visual link to the fields near your home.

COLOR BLENDS

You can achieve a variety of garden effects by subtle blends of color.

soothing harmonies
combine green and white; pink, pastel blue, and lilac; or pale yellow and green

vibrant tones
combine red and yellow; yellow and blue; orange and blue; red and pink against green; or darker yellow and green

an elevating touch
combine pink and golden yellow; yellow and violet; or violet and pink

In a seaside setting, use driftwood or other found objects from the beach to add interest or to build fences. Try growing cultivated forms of the heathers and flowers that add color to local headlands.

In a city garden or roof terrace, consider the colors of surrounding buildings or the hues predominant in the urban view when choosing your color scheme. My patio is overlooked by the cream-white walls of a small office; this color is echoed and set off by the tiny white flowers and green foliage of the climbing jasmine at the garden's end.

Consider adding trelliswork to disguise the perimeter walls of a roof terrace and safeguard its privacy. Scented climbers and flowers will add to the sense of a sky retreat–a safe enclave that shuts out the busy world beneath.

plan for *change*

Your garden allows you to be an artist. The space is a blank canvas, and you have all the colors of flowers, foliage, earth, wood, and brickwork as your palette. But unlike a painter, you have the opportunity to create an ever-changing display of colors and textures. Each season has a characteristic color scheme—from the pinks and primrose yellows of spring through the yellow, white, and bright red joys of summer to the rusty orange and reddish browns of fall and the bare branches and white frosts of winter. Some plant colors summon the spirit of a season—yellow daffodils and forsythia in spring, towering sunflowers or fragrant roses in late summer, astonishing red maples and yellow birches in the fall, and red-berried holly and fir trees in winter.

PLANT YOUR GARDEN FOR ALL-YEAR COLOR

SPRING

Color	Plant	Flowering notes
white and pink	snowdrop (*Galanthus nivalis*)	late winter–early spring
	crocus (*Crocus chrysanthus*)	late winter–early spring
	tulip	spring
	iris	early summer
	English hawthorn (*Crataegus laevigata*)	blossom in late spring
mauve	Canterbury bell (*Campanula medium*)	late spring–midsummer
	Dutch crocus (*Crocus vernus*)	late winter–early spring
yellow	daffodil	early spring
	evening primrose (*Oenothera missouriensis*)	late spring–early summer
	forsythia (shrub) (*Forsythia x intermedia*)	early spring
red–purple	magnolia (shrub) (*Magnolia liliiflora*)	late spring

SUMMER

Color	Plant	Flowering notes
red	dahlia (e.g. 'Scarlet Comet' or 'Alva's Doris')	midsummer–fall
	freesia (e.g. *Freesia x kewensis* 'Madame Curie')	late summer
	oriental poppy (*Papaver orientale*)	early summer–midsummer
	gladiolus (*Gladiolus* 'Sabu')	all summer
pink–white	hollyhock (*Alcea rosea*)	mid–late summer; sometimes fall
	belladonna lily (*Amaryllis belladonna*)	late summer
	azalea (*Rhododendron viscosum*)	early–late summer
orange	montbretia (*Crocosmia masoniorum*)	mid–late summer
mauve–violet	monkshood (*Aconitum wilsonii*)	late summer–early fall
	echinacea (*Echinacea purpurea*)	mid–late summer
	sword lily (*Gladiolus byzantinus*)	midsummer
	Siberian iris (*Iris sibirica*)	early summer
	lupine (*Lupinus polyphyllus*)	midsummer
blue	speedwell (*Veronica spicata*)	mid–late summer
	African lily (*Agapanthus* 'Lilliput')	mid–late summer
yellow–orange	pot marigold (*Calendula officinalis*)	late summer–early fall
	common sunflower (*Helianthus annuus*)	late summer–early fall

FALL

Color	Plant	Flowering notes
pink	New England aster (*Aster novi-belgii*)	late summer–early fall
mauve	Italian aster (*Aster amellus*)	late summer–early fall
yellow–orange	African marigold (*Tagetes erecta*)	throughout summer
evergreen	grasses such as New Zealand flax (*Phormium tenax* 'Variegatum') or yucca (*Yucca filamentosa* 'Variegata')	
red	creeping cotoneaster (*Cotoneaster adpressus*)	dark green-leaved shrub, bears red berries in the fall

WINTER

Color	Plant	Flowering notes
all colors	winter pansies (e.g. *Viola x wittrockiana*)	fall–winter
reds	rosehips (e.g. *Rosa paulii*) cyclamen (*Cyclamen coum*) red-barked dogwood (*Cornus alba* 'Sibirica') red willow (*Salix alba* 'Britzensis')	spring–early summer midwinter–early spring red stems in winter red-orange stems in winter
white–pink	winter cherry (*Prunus x subhirtella* 'Autumnalis')	white or pink flowers in winter
white–yellow	mimosa (*Acacia dealbata*)	silvery leaves and scented yellow flowers winter–spring
green flowers	holly (e.g. *Ilex aquifolium* or *Ilex x altaclerensis*)	white flowers spring–early summer and berries in fall
blue	winter iris (*Iris unguicularis*)	fall–early spring
yellow	mahonia (*Mahonia x media* 'Charity') Chinese witch hazel (*Hamamelis mollis*)	flower clusters in winter flower clusters in midwinter

water and *light*

The play of light adds to the vibrancy and subtlety of the color contrasts created by the plants, trees, and man-made structures in your garden. Different colors predominate in natural light at different times of day (see page 18), affecting the color emphasis of your garden display. And the varying qualities of light during the different seasons and in various weather conditions either suppress or enhance color effects. For example, the hazy light that is characteristic of a hot dusty summer day tends to deaden or dull colors that would sparkle with freshness in the bright, clear light that follows a spring storm.

One way to enhance color in your garden and to introduce form and structure is through the use of shade. All but the most vibrant colors will look bleached in bright sunlight, while dappled shade rests the eyes and enables them to see depth and contrast in lighter hues.

In a very sunny spot, areas of shade created by planting trees or bushes will provide contrast and definition. If your garden is too shady, cut back overhead foliage in a far corner to make an enticing area of dappled light. When light is low toward dusk or at night, create dramatic effects with candles, lanterns, torches, and electric light.

The movements of dappled light and color reflections on water add magic to the garden atmosphere. It is a joy to see the deep red of a climbing rose reflected in a still surface. In a small garden, a pond or fountain can be expensive to install and may require continuing maintenance, but there are simpler alternatives—try a birdbath, for instance, or even a glazed pot or large copper bowl filled with water.

WATERBORNE PLANTS

In the Chinese tradition, the lotus is a plant of summer and signifies purity of spirit. The flower, which blooms for a single day, is also the national flower of India, where religious iconography often depicts the Buddha or the Hindu god Brahma seated on a lotus flower.

An easy alternative to the lotus is to grow a water lily in a good-sized glazed pot filled with water. Keep the pot in partial shade. This is a cheap and easy way to enjoy the calming effects of water in your garden.

LIGHTER AND DARKER

The colors of your garden change as the quality of light varies at different times of day. Light colors such as yellow and white gain an intensely bright appearance under the noon sun, while darker colors are unaffected. White flowers will stand out brilliantly from green foliage.

In the red to violet light of sunset, dark garden hues such as purple and blue appear to grow darker as the light colors, especially white, gain a ghostly luminescence.

CAMERA EYE

Take photographs of your garden in early morning and mid-morning, at noon, in mid- and later afternoon, and in the dying light near dusk. Try again on another day, when the weather is markedly different. The results will reveal how particular areas appear at different times and in different weathers; they may give you ideas of ways to enhance the appearance and color design of parts of the garden—how to bring a distant corner out of obscurity, say, or how to lead the eye across the garden in a smoother or more dramatic movement.

A GARDEN FULL OF LIGHT

There are many ways of using light to enhance your garden color.

Candles set in the earth.

Flame torches.

Glass lanterns hanging from a tree; make your own glass lanterns using food jars, candles, and wire.

Chinese paper lanterns.

Christmas tree lights or larger electric string and rope lights, wound around trees and plant stalks (check that they are safe for outside use); they can also be intertwined in garden structures such as an arbor or trelliswork.

Electric spotlights.

Votive candles in a silver bowl, floating in water in a glass container or floating in a pond.

Spotlight trained on a garden fountain.

Candles, lights, or rope lights set in windows overlooking the garden.

A candelabra or selection of candles arranged on a garden table.

A chiminea (a clay or cast-iron wood- and charcoal-burning oven/patio heater) provides a warm glow.

the *soothing* garden

To create a peaceful garden that offers a retreat from the busy modern world, aim for a harmonious blend of colors. Try white and pastel pink, gentle yellow, cool blue, and elevating violet set against the green of foliage and long grass. Avoid hues that create strong contrasts and offer stimulation, such as vibrant reds, oranges, and bright yellows.

The green of foliage and grasses provides the perfect setting for an array of peaceful colors, balancing their energies and enhancing their soothing effects. Nature's green is constant but subtly changing: it works its magic throughout the year, from the deep evergreen shades of winter and the lighter, more vibrant hues of spring through dusty, sun-drenched summer greens to the dying colors of late summer and early fall, when green fades to yellow and brown. Make room for green—if foliage is crowded out by flowers, the floral colors, however gentle, will begin to banish the sense of peacefulness from your soothing garden.

A PLACE TO SIT

Don't forget to make a place for yourself in your scheme. When planning colors and planting, consider where you will sit to take pleasure in them. Choose a spot where you can look away from the house or flat (and forget the jobs and worries associated with it) to gaze at soothing colors—and enjoy any view you may have of sky, sea, or landscape beyond the garden. If you are choosing flowers for their fragrance as well as their color, plant the sweetest-smelling ones alongside your place of refuge. For example, train a rose up the wall behind your seat or a swathe of lavender near your hammock.

Do you have a tree big enough to hang a simple swing? The soothing effects of the green, dappled shade and the array of flowerbed colors beyond will be enhanced by the gentle movement of air against your face as you swing idly back and forth.

Don't choose style over comfort in garden furniture: some of the elegant metal seats and benches on the market may not be practical—they may be too hard and angular for your body. You can add color and comfort with pillows and drapes.

SOUND AND COLOR

The gentle sounds of nature provide a supportive backdrop for the soothing effects of your garden colors. Contemplative thoughts are enriched by the music of water trickling in a shade-dappled stream or falling in a white spray from a fountain, the call of birds in green leaves, the drone of bees above red and yellow flowers, the rustle of the breeze in the trees against the blue sky. If you don't have a stream, fountain, or tree, you can add sound to color by planting grasses. Their whisper in a breeze at dusk will draw your eye to their delicate greens, blues, and grays. Recommended grasses include needle grass (*Stipa tenuissima*), giant feather grass (*Stipa gigantea*), pheasant's tail grass (*Stipa arundinacea*), *Briza triloba*, and *Carex comans*.

PLANTS FOR A SOOTHING COLOR GARDEN

pink	alpine clematis (*Clematis alpina*) goat's rue (*Galega officinalis*) mallow (*Lavatera trimestris*)
blue	morning glory (*Ipomoea purpurea*) sea holly (*Eryngium bourgatii*) Siberian iris (*Iris sibirica*) Jacob's ladder (*Polemonium foliosissimum*)
violet or purple	lavender (*Lavandula*) Cupid's dart (*Catananche caerulea*) grassy bells (*Edraianthus pumilio*) allium (*Allium sphaerocephalon*)
white or cream	arum lily (*Zantedeschia aethiopica*) bishop's flower (*Ammi majus*) giant snowflake (*Leucojum aestivum* 'Gravetye Giant') masterwort (*Astrantia major*) foxglove (*Digitalis purpurea* f. *albiflora*)
green	lady fern (*Athyrium filix-femina*) alpine water fern (*Blechnum penna-marina*) Japanese holly fern (*Cyrtomium fortunei*) broad buckler fern (*Dryopteris dilatata*) ostrich fern (*Matteuccia struthiopteris*)

the *vibrant* garden

To create a stimulating outdoor space that will give you restorative bursts of energy, plant red, deep yellow, and orange—poppies, peonies, tulips, sunflowers, montbretia, and daffodils. The effect can be achieved as much by the planting as the plants themselves—a wide flowerbed of densely colored tulips, say, with a few balancing greens, will certainly lift rather than soothe your spirits. A stand of sunflowers crowded in a sun-drenched corner or a white garden wall covered in red roses will have the same effect.

EXPRESSING YOUR ASPIRATIONS

A corner of your garden that is dominated by green, blue, and pink expresses your existing sense of calm, but also helps to create inner security—merely visiting the spot and drinking in the vibrations of these soothing colors will enable you to find a quiet, restorative space in a mind full of turmoil. In the same way, more stimulating areas of color are an expression of the levels of energy and vibrant self-confidence to which you aspire. A few moments in this bright garden corner should provide the pick-me-up you need.

A well-planned, carefully maintained plot—which includes elements of symmetry, perhaps with a pond or other water feature and harmonious use of colors—provides an example of order and stability that you can turn to when life beyond the home seems chaotic.

A more unrestrained garden landscape—with irregular plantings of wildflowers and grasses, and a backdrop of trees or shrubs—is an example of the rolling movement of the seasons, of the earth's irrepressible fecundity. If modern life seems sterile or trivial, you may find inspiration in this vision of a natural order that carries on as it always has done.

LANGUAGE OF FLOWERS

In past centuries, lovers, friends, and relatives understood the meanings associated with gifts of particular blooms. We still associate red roses with declarations of love but have forgotten many other traditional floral meanings.

chrysanthemums
signify friendship.

irises
are associated with wisdom.

**white lilies and
white violets**
represent innocence.

white carnations
mean the best of luck.

**blue forget-me-nots
and white daisies**
signify faithfulness.

pansies
convey enduring love.

**orange blossom
and marjoram**
are linked with fertility

honeysuckle
means a secret love.

marigolds
represent a shared sadness.

PLANTS FOR A VIBRANT GARDEN

red	Peruvian lily (*Alstroemeria aurantiaca*) cinquefoil (*Potentilla* 'Gibson's Scarlet') *Ricinus communis* 'Carmencita' montbretia (*Crocosmia* 'Lucifer')
yellow	daffodil, yellow tulip, sunflower evening primrose (*Oenothera missouriensis*) Jerusalem sage (*Phlomis fruticosa*) Spanish broom (*Genista lydia*) winter aconite (*Eranthis hyemalis*)
orange	canna lily (*Canna* 'Wyoming') English marigold (*Calendula officinalis* 'Indian Prince') California poppy (*Eschscholzia californica*) African marigold (*Tagetes erecta*)

VIBRANT TREES AND SHRUBS

To make a dramatic impact in your garden, plant one or more of the following trees or shrubs.

Chilean fire bush
(*Embothrium coccineum*)
Evergreen that produces scarlet-orange flowers in the first half of summer; grows up to 30 feet (9 meters) in height.

Laburnum
(*Laburnum anagyroides*)
Tree that produces golden-yellow flowers in spring and summer; grows up to 18 feet (4 meters).

Common broom
(*Cytisus scoparius*)
Shrub that produces deep yellow flowers in the early months of summer; grows up to 6 feet (1.8 meters).

Variegated weigela
(*Weigela florida* 'Aureovariegata')
Shrub that flowers pink in summer; grows up to 6 feet 6 inches (2 meters).

Cinquefoil
(*Potentilla arbuscula*)
Shrub that produces yellow flowers from late spring to end of fall; grows up to 4 feet (1.2 meters).

IN HARMONY WITH YOUR HOME

A naturalized garden that incorporates local wildflowers, plants that attract birds, butterflies, and other wildlife, and is designed to complement its surroundings will affirm your sense of being in the right place at the right time, reminding you that you belong there and have much to offer in life.

color all *around*

Color in your garden derives not just from plants and vegetation. Consider the hues and textures of your garden walls and fences, of garden furniture, children's play equipment, sheds, decking, paving, tiles, statues, tubs, pots, areas of gravel or stones—and perhaps a summerhouse, treehouse, or birds' nesting box. All contribute to the overall color scheme. The colors of the building in which you live— porch, window frames, shutters, roof material, chimney blocks, guttering and drainpipes, windowboxes, wall baskets—affect your color response in the garden. And the colors you can see when you look out from the garden are also influential: trees or bushes on a nearby plot of land, climbing plants on your neighbor's wall, a sea or country view, or the predominant hues of an urban landscape.

NEIGHBOR CLASH

If you live close to your neighbors, the decorative scheme on the front and back of their houses will have an impact on the way you experience color in your garden. If your neighbor's house or paintwork clashes with your own house or garden color scheme, consider repainting or replanting to create harmony. Alternatively, plant a climber or tree at the edge of your plot to introduce the harmonizing influence of its foliage and flowers and to dilute the color clash.

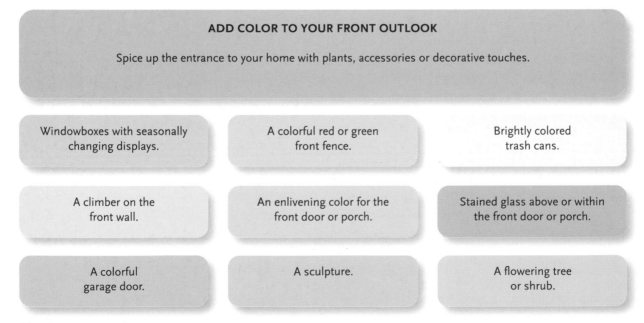

ADD COLOR TO YOUR FRONT OUTLOOK

Spice up the entrance to your home with plants, accessories or decorative touches.

Windowboxes with seasonally changing displays.	A colorful red or green front fence.	Brightly colored trash cans.
A climber on the front wall.	An enlivening color for the front door or porch.	Stained glass above or within the front door or porch.
A colorful garage door.	A sculpture.	A flowering tree or shrub.

WATER MIRROR

If you have a pool, fountain, or swimming pool, the color decisions you make in respect of tiling, fixtures, and surroundings will have lasting impact. Remember that still water reflects and tends to take on the color of whatever lies above and around it—the blue of sky, the green of surrounding or overhanging trees. Shallow water will also take color from any tiles visible through it. Try turquoise-green, blue, or red-pink tiles—and plant harmoniously in the surrounding area. If you plan to illuminate a fountain with a spotlight, experiment with colored bulbs.

FRONT APPROACH

Many of us have functional front yards—places to park the car or store the bicycle, to keep refuse cans, and so on. A drab outlook may subtly drag you down each time you return home, or project an unwelcoming, depressing image of your home to visitors and passersby. Consider also how well the color of your driveway harmonizes with the front of the house, and how well any wall or fencing at the front of your property combines with the driveway, the front-yard colors, and the house itself.

GARDEN ART

A statue, an arrangement of stones, or a wooden carving add color to a garden and can greatly enhance its atmosphere. Oriental busts and statues of the Buddha, a bodhisattva, or some Hindu gods and goddesses bring a serene presence. Consider color and impact when deciding where to place your artwork—a green-tinged statue clearly may not have much of an impact when set against foliage; you may prefer to stand it in a hidden place around a corner or behind an outgrowth of vegetation so that visitors to the garden come upon it unexpectedly. Sometimes you will be guided by tradition—images of the elephant-headed Hindu god Ganesha, "Lord of the Threshold," are often set above or alongside doorways.

TREE WISDOM

According to ancient Chinese wisdom, evergreens indicate that you will live a long time, apple trees are the sign of a safe haven, and orange trees bring good luck.

color and *fragrance*

The fragrance of flowers is an important part of the beauty of your garden, their heady scents bringing back happy memories, reviving the spirits and metaphorically transporting you to a peaceful, revitalizing place. You may grow some less attractive plants such as mignonette for their scent alone, but if you are seeking to combine color and fragrance, there is a wide selection of flowers to choose from.

Many beautifully scented plants have predominantly white flowers—honeysuckle, jasmine, lilies, or white roses make a pleasing contrast against the green leaves of foliage or an expanse of brickwork behind. Pink sweet pea or the distinctive sweep of lavender add contrasting color. Experiment with planting flowers that combine fragrances: lilies, roses, and honeysuckle set against a green garden corner make a seductive combination of scents.

A small herb garden or a few herbs grown among flowers will enhance your blend of colors and scents—and the herbs will also be

useful in the kitchen. An area of purple-flowering thyme or soothing green sage adds a new dimension to your garden, while spiky rosemary or feathery fennel make for an intriguing contrast of texture set against other plants.

You can plan your colored and perfumed garden to deliver evocative fragrances from beautiful flowers throughout the year. In winter the scented and yellow-flowering witch hazel and wintersweet will add arresting scents and a splash of color even on the darkest days. *Mahonia japonica* combines the appeal of reddish-purple leaves with lemon-colored flowers and a scent that resembles lily of the valley.

If you have a large garden, plant your winter-flowering shrubs near the house or alongside a pathway that you frequently use so you will get the most from them even at times when the weather discourages you from spending much time outside.

In spring try *Daphne odora* 'Aureomarginata,' which offers highly scented red-purple flowers backed by yellow-edged evergreen leaves. In later spring and early summer, try *Gardenia jasminoides*, which has white-to-yellow flowers with a sweet fragrance that are set off delightfully against the plant's glossy dark green leaves. Once again, plant them toward the front of the plot, near a path, so that you can enjoy the full effect of the fragrance.

Colorful scented flowers for summer include red-to-purple peonies, pink border phlox, and creamy-white mock orange. If you take pleasure in evocatively scented walks at dusk, try pinkish night-scented stock, whose flowers open in the evening. For a beautifully scented rose, try the intensely sweet-fragranced *Rosa gallica* var. *officinalis*.

The remarkable power of scents to recall memories and evoke feelings means that you should take care when selecting plants for their fragrance. A particular scent may be enough to transport you back to a time of heartbreak or bereavement—and, if so, you would not want to be reminded of this difficult period every day in your garden. Before buying and planting, pause to consider and, if necessary, check the scents of flowers and herbs.

For maximum effect, grow scented flowers in a sunny, sheltered corner of the garden, where no breeze is likely to dissipate the perfume. If you can, visit your scented garden in the morning when the dew-fresh flowers are at their most fragrant. Train plants over arches and arbors so that their scent is released above you and hangs in the air. Place a bench or chair nearby so that you can take your ease in that precious spot, bathed in the soothing and restorative combination of hues and fragrances.

PLANTS THAT COMBINE COLOR AND FRAGRANCE

border phlox
(*Phlox paniculata*)

common thyme
(*Thymus vulgaris*)

Daphne odora
'Aureomarginata'

lavender
(*Lavandula*)

night-scented stock
(*Matthiola bicornis*)

peony
(*Paeonia lactiflora*)

scented varieties of rose

sweet rocket
(*Hesperis matronalis*)

wintersweet
(*Chimonanthus praecox*)

witch hazel
(*Hamamelis*)

color and *nutrition*

food *colors* and a *balanced* diet

Color stimulates our appetite for healthy food. Nature brings a rich array of color to our tables: the deep red of a tomato, the purple of an eggplant, the fresh yellow of a lemon, the variegated greens of a bowl of salad leaves, the golden brown of the crust on freshly baked bread. In food preparation and nutrition—as in clothes, gardening, and throughout the home—natural colors deliver goodness, healing, and vitalizing energy.

COLOR NUTRITION

Color nutrition works by applying the spectrum of the rainbow to diet— from red and orange (red meat, peaches) through gold/yellow (rice, wholegrains, bananas) and green (lettuce, peas, kiwi fruit) to blue-violet (olives, plums, beets). Monitor the color range of the foods you normally eat. If your usual foods are predominantly one color, you probably need to broaden your diet to make sure your body receives a well-balanced combination of nutrients.

GETTING THE MOST FROM FOOD

Eat food lightly cooked or raw to obtain the maximum benefit from its color and nutritional content. Overcooking vegetables destroys their color, vitamins, and minerals—compare the color of freshly grated carrot with the sliced carrots often served in mass-catering establishments. Purchase only the freshest organic ingredients to avoid unnatural chemical additives. Cook vegetables by steaming, rather than boiling, to preserve their fresh color and nutritional goodness. Use food shortly after you buy it or pick it—if possible, bring it to your table direct from your garden. Prepare your food just before you eat it; research has shown that the longer you store prepared vegetables, say, the more it reduces their nutritional value. Finally, don't rush. Give the food your full attention as you prepare and eat it. Let your heart fill with love for the family or friends with whom you will share the meal.

NATURAL OR SYNTHETIC?

Food manufacturers know how much color appeals to us, and use bright synthetic hues to make processed foods appear appetizing–think of the garish colors of some ice cream and fast foods. In this respect, our love of color can lead us astray. These chemical colors may be attractive, but do not necessarily provide the kind of nourishment we need. For the sake of our health, we must learn to distinguish between natural and synthetic colors.

THE RAINBOW COLORS OF A BALANCED DIET

If you have a good mixture of food colors in your diet, you will maintain a balanced intake— thereby increasing your vitality and helping to safeguard your health.

about half of food intake should be from the mid-range of the spectrum
gold/brown to green; make up the rest with blue/indigo, purple, and red foods.

a healthy meal will include foods that are gold/brown, green, and red/orange
for example, chicken breast with carrots and red pepper (red/orange), potatoes (gold/brown), and broccoli with peas and beans (green). Red and white meats are usually classified as red foods.

for a balanced diet you should add some blue, indigo, and purple foods
perhaps a dish of blackberries, black cherries, and red-purple grapes.

the color nutrition scheme is easily adapted to your dietary needs
replace chicken with cheese if you are vegetarian, or with lentils if you are vegan.

warming foods, *cooling* foods

YIN	YANG
female	male
earth	sky
valley	mountain
passive	active
dark	light
absorbing	penetrating
sweet	salty
moist	dry
cool	hot

Some foods have a warming and drying effect, while others are comparatively cooling and moistening. In terms of color nutrition, warming foods are at the red end of the spectrum and cooling foods are towards the blue end. The traditional Chinese theory of yin and yang adds to our understanding of these differences.

From ancient times, the Chinese explained the universe in terms of the complementary yin and yang principles. The two principles are part of a continuum. Everything, including food and color, is at a point on this continuum—is more or less yin or yang.

YIN-YANG AND COLOR
The yin-yang continuum can be overlaid on the color spectrum. Yin corresponds to the blue end of the spectrum and yang to red—yin is particularly linked to azure blue and yang to orange. Foods are yin, yang, or "balancing." The balancing foods occupy a position in the center of the continuum and are associated mainly with green. Yin foods are blue-violet foods and drinks such as honey, sugar, alcohol, and milk. Balancing foods are golden yellow and green foods such as cereals, nuts, seeds, and vegetables. Yang foods are red-orange foods including red meat, eggs, cheese, and salt.

HEALTH FOOD
Using foods from different color groups is one way to boost your reserves of color energy. Try to be sensitive to your body's needs: this approach may help protect against some physical ailments—and perhaps jump-start your self-confidence and optimism to help to combat psychological difficulties such as depression. Foods from the red-orange-yellow end of the spectrum provide a warming lift and boost brainpower. Green foods bring harmony to an individual's color energy. Blue-violet foods may ease muscular pains and soothe problems associated with constriction and anxiety.

LOOK FOR HEALTHY COLORS

If we encourage children to take pleasure in the natural colors of the foods they eat, they are more likely to learn to associate natural colors with things that taste good and to appreciate a healthy nutritional and color balance in their diet.

FEELING BLUE?

To keep healthy and feeling our best, we need to maintain a balance of yin and yang in our body and in our diet. Too much yin may make a person feel depressed, while too much yang may be associated with overheating or heart and circulation problems. Good health depends on a balance between yin and yang. Once this balance is achieved, our body's immune system should be strong and naturally keep illness at bay.

SINGLE-COLOR BOOST

If you are drawn to one color energy at a particular time, try creating a plate of food in that color. (Color nutritionists categorize canned fish and milk products as green foods.)

green
Tuna and avocado with green beans and lettuce salad, followed by green grapes.

yellow-orange
Rice with yellow lentils, butternut squash and potato cooked in ginger and turmeric, followed by an orange and mango fruit salad.

red
Lean rare steak, red lentils, kidney beans, and red peppers, served with cooked tomatoes, followed by a salad of raspberries, cranberries, and strawberries.

blue-indigo-violet
Grilled eggplant with red-purple rice garnished with radicchio, accompanied by beet salad, followed by blueberries.

FIVE FOODS FOR A COLD DAY
pumpkin soup
a meal made with hot spices, such as chile and ginger
grilled red pepper
peach
raspberries

FIVE FOODS FOR A WARM DAY
eggplant
beansprouts
cucumber
grapefruit
banana

green foods

◗ ◗ ◗

GREEN REMEDY

If you are under great stress or have recently had a nasty shock such as an accident, you may be in need of green-energy foods. You can boost the effect of the foods on your body and spirit by drinking green-energized water (see pages 132–3) and by wearing a green pullover or scarf.

Green is the color of balance. Gentle greens are linked to the heart chakra (see page 121), and associated with love, forgiveness, and a sense of security, with finding a calm and evenhanded way between extremes.

When we combine foods by color, we use leafy vegetables and other green-energy sources to balance the force of foods from the red/orange/yellow group such as red meat, pasta, and cheese and those from the blue/violet group such as fresh fish, mushrooms, and soy. If we imagine a meal as a rainbow on a plate, then green foods are the essential middle wavelength that balances and connects the red/orange and blue/violet bands on either side.

Many vegetables and fruits clearly contain green energy—for example, cabbage, lettuce, peas, avocados, broccoli, green beans, zucchini, green peppers, brussel sprouts, green apples, grapes, kiwi fruits, limes, spring greens, and so on. But not all green-energy foods are green in color. In addition to leafy greens and other vegetables, green-energy foods include canned fish such as tuna and sardines; olive oil, olives, and nuts; tofu and some beans and legumes; and milk and yogurt, both of which are understood to be green in origin, since animals eat grass or other green foods while making their milk.

YOUR BODY'S GUIDANCE

The most beneficial way to decide which foods to choose and how to balance their colors is to listen to your body and let it tell you what it needs. You may have to take a step out of the daily round, perhaps by embarking on a 24-hour fast or following a detox diet, in order to break the force of dietary habits that might otherwise confuse you.

Experiment with different foods and different combinations of the color-energy groups and note the effects on your energy levels, your digestion, and your overall sense of physical and spiritual wellbeing.

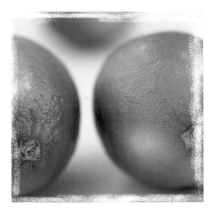

BENEFITS OF GREEN FOODS

Green vegetables have a cleansing effect on the body, making them ideal for a natural detox. Green foods can also have beneficial effects on blood pressure and stomach acidity. On a psychological plane, green foods foster harmony in life.

GREEN ENERGY: MAKE TIME FOR OTHERS

Many of us suffer from competing demands in our lives, leaving us regretful that we cannot spend more energy on our children or on a private project that we care passionately about. But when we can achieve color balance, when we have an abundance of middle-wavelength green energy, we begin to find harmony between different parts of our life—or to understand how to bring about a harmonious resolution to our problems. This new insight liberates time that we can then devote to other people. Green is also the color of love, forgiveness, and self-confidence—solidly grounded in green energy, with a healthy heart and a cooperative nature and well-established in ourselves, we have the confidence and time to look outward and can make ourselves available to respond to the pressing needs of a troubled world.

yellow and *orange* foods

EAT YELLOW

In foods, yellow ranges from the rich shades of a banana skin or a slab of salty butter to the thinner, greener hues of lemon. Yellow foods include many staples of a healthy diet: rice, wholegrains, nuts, yellow lentils, corn, butter, lemon, banana, pineapple, melon, and grapefruit.

Someone who is feeling lethargic or depressed can be helped by a burst of the uplifting energy contained in orange and yellow foods. Try these color vibrations if you are suffering from lack of sunlight in winter, are run down by overwork, or are fearful of facing a new challenge.

Yellow is the color of the solar plexus chakra or energy center, which is believed by color nutritionists to govern the body's digestive and nervous systems. The yellow color vibration fosters clear thinking, confidence, and a positive outlook. (See pages 1120–1 and page 126 for a full explanation of the body's chakras.)

Orange is the color of the sacral chakra, which governs both the stomach and the reproductive system. Orange appears to enhance our appetite for food, which is why it is frequently used in the decoration of restaurants and is recommended as part of a balanced color scheme for a dining area in the home. The color is also believed to promote fertility. The orange color vibration helps us to feel confident, capable, sociable, and communicative.

BENEFITS OF YELLOW AND ORANGE FOODS

Many orange and yellow foods contain antioxidants, which can protect against serious disease.

- The body requires beta-carotene, found in carrots and in green and other orange-yellow vegetables and fruits, to make vitamin A. Vitamin A boosts the immune system and helps us to maintain healthy skin and eyes.
- Vitamin A and vitamin C: Found abundantly in oranges and lemons, as well as in green vegetables. Important antioxidants (see page 109) that can offer protection against heart disease and cancer.
- Vitamin E: Found in yellow foods such as wholegrains, seeds, and nuts. Helps to protect against heart disease, certain cancers, and other chronic ailments, and may slow the effects of aging.
- Orange and yellow foods enhance the body's capacity to break foods down and expel waste products.
- Yellow color energy may improve the memory as well as other thought processes.
- Orange color energy may help us to take pleasure in life—enjoying food and social interaction, while benefiting from a healthy libido.
- The positive attitude fostered by these colors helps to protect against self-destructive patterns of thought and behavior. Optimism and self-belief are a great benefit when we need to recover from an illness, injury, or other setback.

EAT ORANGE

Fruits, root vegetables, spices, and egg yolks are rich in orange energy. Orange foods include apricot, orange, peach, mango, potato, pasta, carrot, rutabaga, pumpkin, ginger, butternut squash, and turmeric.

red foods

Many of the most enticing fruits and vegetables are bright reds that conjure visions of a crisp and colorful alfresco lunch on a sun-baked summer's day. The many natural reds of raspberries, strawberries, red cherries, watermelon, tomatoes, radishes, and red peppers bear witness to the goodness of sun-ripened, vitamin-rich food.

Red color in food may also mean hearty winter meals of roast beef for carnivores, or platefuls of red lentils with grilled peppers for vegetarians and vegans. Meats and most other animal products are considered by color nutritionists to be foods filled with red energy.

Red in food has a stimulating, energizing power. It is the color of the lowest of the body's chakras or energy centers, the base chakra, situated at the base of the spine. It governs the kidneys and the system of muscles (see page 121).

PROS AND CONS OF RED FOODS

Red can boost our strength and vitality, making us determined and filling us with primal energy. However, certain red-energy foods can lead to overstimulation. If we eat an excess of them, we risk becoming overexcited, short-tempered, and impatient; we may find it difficult to settle to work; we may begin to rush when we should go slowly and carefully. The solution is to seek balance by adding golden yellow and green foods to the table.

Some brightly colored fruits, such as red yew berries, are poisonous, and rotting food sometimes grows bright molds, but the fresh color of a fruit or vegetable usually signals that the food will help to safeguard health.

HOT TOMATOES

A diet rich in lycopene—a type of carotenoid found in large quantities in cooked tomatoes—reduces a man's risk of developing prostate cancer by almost 45 percent.

But salad tomatoes do not deliver an equivalent benefit— there is five times more lycopene in cooked tomatoes than in raw ones.

FREE RADICALS AND ANTIOXIDANTS

After every meal, as our digestive system breaks down the food we have eaten, our body produces unstable molecules called free radicals, which react with nearby molecules, setting off a process called oxidation, which can have many harmful effects on health. For example, oxidation in the blood can result in the buildup of fatty deposits, which can eventually lead to stroke or heart disease. Oxidation in the nucleus of a cell can trigger changes that lead to cancer. Research has also linked the activity of free radicals with premature aging and the development of arthritis and cataracts.

Antioxidants are natural substances found in some foods that are used by the body as protection against free radicals. Vitamins A, C, and E and carotenoids—pigments that give fruit and vegetables their deep red, yellow, and orange colors—are examples of antioxidants. Eating fruits and vegetables rich in carotenoids and vitamins A, C, and E gives the body plenty of antioxidants to fight disease. There are six types of carotenoid used by the body to maintain health (see chart below).

FOODS RICH IN ANTIOXIDANTS

Antioxidant type	Food color group	Found most commonly in
alpha-carotene	orange	carrots, pumpkins
beta-carotene	orange/yellow/red/green	carrots, red peppers, red and green fruits
cryptoxanthin	orange	peaches, oranges
lutein, zeaxanthin	green/red/orange	leafy greens, pumpkins, red peppers
lycopene	red	cooked tomatoes, watermelons
vitamin A	red/yellow/orange	apples, red peppers, butter, egg yolk, liver
vitamin C	red/yellow/orange/green	oranges, lemons, strawberries, cherries, red peppers, leafy greens
vitamin E	yellow	wholegrains, nuts

blue, indigo, and *violet* foods

Foods that come from the blue-indigo to violet end of the spectrum tend to have a cooling rather than a stimulating effect. Blues contain a preponderance of yin over yang energy (see page 102). Blue food suggests first of all berries and plums–fruits such as blackberries, blueberries, black cherries, and raisins. Color nutritionists also consider mushrooms, olives, yeast, soybeans, and most fish to be blue.

Blue is the color of the throat chakra (see page 121) or energy center and controls the respiratory system. You may benefit from the energy of blue food if you feel confused or anxious. Blue will help you to relax and breathe more easily, delivering the confidence of self-possession and the power of imagination. Blue food energy may help you slow yourself down to a more productive speed if your anxiety is forcing you to rush things.

Purple-violet foods include eggplant, beets, radicchio, purple cabbage, and suitably colored plums, onions, peppers, and cabbage. They mix the heating, stimulating vibration of red with the cooling, more peaceful vibration of blue to create a balanced energy that combines yang (red) and yin (blue).

Violet is the color of the crown chakra, at the very top of the head, which controls

---

SPICES, HERBS, AND COLOR ENERGIES

Spices and herbs bring a wide variety of blue and other color energies to the table through their use in cooking.

Spice or Herb	Color	Suggested Use
poppy seeds (from *Papaver somniferum*)	blue-gray	use to add nutty taste and aroma to breads, rolls, Turkish desserts
cilantro (seed of *Coriandrum sativum*)	yellow-red	use in curries
ginger (root of *Zingiber officinale*)	golden yellow, brown	use in curries, ginger ale, or gingerbread
sage (leaves of *Salvia officinalis*)	gray-green	use when cooking with meat, chopped in salads, or with cheese
oregano (leaves of *Origanum vulgare*)	green	use in pizza and chile powder

HERBAL HEALING

Purple-blue-indigo herbs and herbs of other colors deliver healing through their use in natural remedies.

Color	Herb	Suggested Use
purple-violet	hyssop (*Hyssopus officinalis*)	to treat breathing problems, help digestion, soothe skin sores
	lavender (*Lavandula officinalis*)	to treat an upset stomach
blue	juniper (*Juniperus communis*)	berries act as a diuretic
pink-red	valerian (*Valeriana officinalis*)	as a mild sedative, especially to encourage sleep
green	aloe vera (*Aloe barbadensis*)	to heal burned skin and soften and sooth skin tissue
yellow	dandelion (*Taraxacum officinale*)	to treat liver problems or stimulate the appetite; acts as a diuretic
	evening primrose (*Oenothera biennis*)	to lower blood pressure; oil from the plant's seeds can be swallowed to treat migraine or types of asthma or eczema
yellow-white	feverfew (*Tanacetum parthenium*)	to treat headaches, insect bites, or migraine
brown-green	witch hazel (*Hamamelis virginiana*)	leaves and bark can be used to treat mild skin conditions

the central nervous system (the brain and the spinal cord). The balanced red-blue energy of violet foods can alleviate stress. The violet, blue, and indigo color vibrations may ease insomnia or problems of the nerves.

FOR YOUR NERVOUS SYSTEM
Essential acids in fish (blue) are beneficial. Eat plenty of oats (violet), which are a tonic for the nerves. Bilberries and blueberries are also recommended.

INDIGO RICE
"Purple sticky rice" from Thailand does not look very appealing in the jar, but it turns an attractive indigo blue once it has been cooked. The rice is usually served as a dessert in rice pudding or rice balls.

JUNIPER HEALING
Native Americans traditionally drank tea made from blue-black juniper berries to ease the symptoms of arthritis and the common cold. They also used the berry to treat stomachaches.

EAT PURPLE-VIOLET

Purple-violet foods include eggplants, shellfish, oats, figs, dates, red cabbage, radicchio, beets, plums, purple onions, and purple broccoli.

adding *color* to the *table*

When you are serving food, it is beneficial to lay the table with care. The ambience in which you eat affects your receptiveness to the food's color energy. The color of the walls and quality of light in your dining area, the degree of comfort, the color of the china, glassware, and table settings—all combine to increase or lessen your appreciation of the food's colors.

In a cafeteria or fast-food outlet you may feel ill at ease seated at a plastic table under a harsh light. The flickering artificial light strips your food of its color. The hard chair or bench on which you sit makes you want to get the meal over quickly—encouraging you, perhaps, to gulp down the food without chewing it carefully or appreciating its texture and aroma or the color combinations it makes on the plate.

But in a comfortably furnished dining room—where your host has chosen a tablecloth that combines pleasingly with the colors of the walls, used lit candles to create an intimate and relaxing atmosphere, and selected plates, glasses, and serving dishes that set off the quality of the food colors—you will find it much easier to take your time and savor the flavors, aromas and color combinations of your meal.

DISHES

White plates contribute the perfect background to a riot of color—for example, the varied greens and reds of a plateful of salad. Conversely, a red earthenware dish will enhance the appeal of a white mound of mashed potatoes or basmati rice. Consider serving a single-color helping on a dish of a complementary color—apricots on a blue plate or a green dish for a plateful of tomatoes.

FLOWER DISPLAY

A vase of freshly picked flowers adds a dash of color, aroma, and interest to mealtimes. Try to put fresh flowers in your dining area as often as possible, rather than simply reserving them for special occasions. You and your family will receive an energy boost from a lively orange and yellow display at breakfast time, say, raising your spirits and helping you prepare to go out and take on the world.

GARNISH

The simplest way to add color to a main meal is with a side garnish—green lettuce, red tomato, a yellow slice of lemon, or a handful of berries.

KITCHEN HERBS

If you do not have room for an herb garden, a few potted herbs will add color and fragrance to your kitchen—and be on hand for cooking. If you do have an herb garden, pick a few plants and try using them in place of flowers for a dining-table display.

ALFRESCO DINING

If you have a yard with available space, consider investing in outdoor dining furniture. In summer, a restful evening meal or shady lunch outside enables your body—bathed in full-spectrum natural light and caressed by the aromas, sounds, and varied hues of your garden—to gain maximum benefit from the color energy of the meal.

DINING COLOR

When preparing a table, consider the colors of the following combined with each other and with the food you are serving.

Decoration of dining area—walls, carpet, chairs, curtains, pictures

Table, tablecloth, placemats.

Napkins and napkin rings.

Salt and pepper dispensers.

Flatware and dishes.

Any jars to be set on the table.

Glass or other serving dishes and bowls.

Glasses, decanters, and pitchers.

Bottles containing drinks.

Flower vases and displays.

Lamps or candlesticks, colored bulbs, and candles.

Effects of natural light and any outside view from the dining area.

chapter 6

color, health, and wellbeing

sensitivity to *light*

Color is a powerful tool for protecting or restoring physical, mental, and spiritual health. The visible rainbow colors are a form of energy, one part of the electromagnetic spectrum of radiation (see pages 10–11). If we understand how this energy can be harnessed, color can be used to treat health and behavioral problems that derive from delicate imbalances in the body.

We receive color energy through the skin as well as through the eyes (see page 12); all our skin cells are sensitive to and responsive to light. The color energy in light is drawn into organs, glands, and body systems primarily through the body's seven main chakras or energy centers (see pages 120–21). Color therapists perceive illness and disease as an imbalance in the color vibration specific to a body system, gland, organ, or other part.

We can use treatment with colored light, with color-energized water or with powerful visualizations of color to boost our immune and other body systems, soothe a stiff shoulder or other area of discomfort, ease depression or clarify our thoughts. We can also use it

WINTER BLUES

If you live in a part of the world where the days are short and the weather is often gloomy in winter, lack of daylight can have an adverse effect on your moods and energy levels.

Make sure that you go outside for around 30 minutes each day, to reap the benefit of the colors in full-spectrum daylight.

Even in the worst weather, wrap up warmly and try to take the air and drink in the light.

When you are inside, sit close to a window. Pull up the blind, draw back the curtains, and let in as much light as possible.

The medical name for problems caused by lack of natural daylight in winter is seasonal affective disorder (SAD). Some sufferers have mild depression, others find it hard to function normally—for example, they often want to stay in bed, they avoid socializing and tend to overeat. SAD is thought to affect at least 10 percent of people in northern Europe each year.

to foster confidence or other qualities to which we aspire, or to dissolve aggression, banish anxiety, and achieve spiritual peace.

LIGHT, SEASONS, AND MOOD

Color and light have profound effects on energy and mood. We perceive colors because light rays stimulate the cells in the eye to despatch nerve impulses to the brain's visual cortex (see page 12). Light-derived impulses also travel to the pineal gland, which determines sleep/wakefulness and other biorhythms, and the pituitary gland, which controls the release of hormones governing mood and many body functions.

COLOR THERAPY IN THE ANCIENT WORLD

The healing power of colored light was deeply respected by the ancient Egyptians. They poured liquids into colored glass jars and bottles, then placed them in full daylight–the light, colored by the container, filled the contents with color energy. They also used colored gems in healing: a person needing the healing vibration of a particular color would ingest a powder made by grinding up a stone of that color.

KEYS TO THE SPIRIT

If you are seeking to enhance a certain personal quality, use this checklist to see which colors can benefit you.

confidence
Yellow or orange will help you to attain your full spiritual stature.

self-discipline
Green, a source of balance and harmony, offers a way between the extremes of self-indulgence and asceticism.

contact with your higher self
Indigo or violet will clarify your thoughts and inspire you to lay aside what is standing between you and your spirit; magenta fosters spiritual yearning.

energy
Red will energize you to work with force and stamina.

creativity
Yellow improves alertness; indigo or violet fosters intuition.

communication
Orange unleashes the warmth and joy that are crucial to working successfully with others; blue harnesses communicative skills.

the *energy* of *color*

Your body is surrounded by a field of electromagnetic energy called the aura, which both draws in and emits color energy. Some people can see the aura as an egg-shaped sheath of colors around the body, and specialized Kirlian photography is said to be able to capture energy flow and reproduce the aura. We are all sensitive to one another's aura energy, although we cannot all see the aura itself.

Humans derive energy from light as well as from food. You have seven main energy centers or chakras on your body, arranged vertically between the base of your spine and the top of your skull. The chakras draw color energy from full-spectrum light through the aura for the body's use. Each of the seven main chakras is attuned to one of the rainbow colors. The theory of the chakras derives from esoteric forms of Hinduism. The word chakra comes from the Sanskrit chakrum, meaning wheel: the chakras are understood to be constantly spinning, and are sometimes likened to flowers endlessly opening and closing. There are said to be 88,000 chakras on the body, but the seven identified here are the most important. They are as follows: the base chakra, the sacral chakra, the solar plexus chakra, the heart chakra, the throat chakra, the brow chakra, and the crown chakra.

YOUR BODY'S CHAKRAS

At the main chakras, your spiritual being and your physical body connect and interact. Each chakra governs a particular body system and organs (see page 114). Each is also associated with areas of self-expression and with physical, mental, and spiritual qualities.

Chakra	Color	Governs
base (base of spine)	red	physical survival, instinct, will, energy, vitality
sacral (below the navel)	orange	sexuality, hunger, social interaction
solar plexus (above the navel)	yellow	intellect, confidence, ego, self-control, optimism
heart (central chest)	green	balance, compassion for others and for self, love, self-security, forgiveness
throat (throat)	blue	creativity, speaking, self-expression
brow (central forehead, "third eye")	indigo	intuitive thought, spiritual insight, self-knowledge
crown (above the crown of the head)	violet	higher spiritual knowledge, transcendence of self, access to deep inner divinity

SENSING THE AURA

We may sometimes have an immediate response to people based not on what they say or their physical appearance. We might feel uncomfortable around those individuals or disturbed by their presence, despite the fact that they may be saying kind words. At these times we may be detecting and responding to disturbances in those people's auras.

CONVINCE YOURSELF

Our knowledge of the chakras and the aura is derived from ancient wisdom—modern medical science does not accept their existence. Follow your own experience. As you progress in attuning your body to color and become convinced of the restorative healing power of color vibrations, the idea that we are surrounded by and emit a field of color energy does not seem outlandish or improbable.

YOUR COLORED CLOAK

A healthy aura operates as a protective shield, keeping negative energy at bay. As we develop greater sensitivity to our body's needs for color energy, we will simultaneously make sure that the chakras are rich in their color vibrations and that our aura is radiant. Strong in ourselves, we will be able to provide for the needs of those around us.

ETHERIC CHAKRA

Some therapists describe an eighth chakra, the etheric, which exists in the aura directly above the crown chakra at the top of the head. It is attuned to magenta, the color that unites the two ends of the color spectrum by blending violet and red.

THE AURA AND HEALTH

Balance is the key to health. An imbalance in the colors or energy of one chakra will have consequent effects on the energy and colors of the other chakras. Some color healers can view the aura to diagnose energy imbalances and future physical ailments.

If your chakras are functioning well, receiving and distributing color energy freely through your body, your physical, mental, and spiritual health will be at an optimum level.

When your chakras are healthy, your aura emits all the colors of the rainbow.

If one or more of your chakras is blocked, or you are depleted in the color energy associated with a particular chakra, then the aura will emit an unbalanced and muddy mixture of colors—often with a preponderance of blue and green. This unbalanced energy may eventually manifest itself as physical disease.

color you

Each of the main chakras governs a set of organs or a body system, and the color vibration linked with a particular chakra benefits that chakra's associated organs and body system. These correspondences are your guide when you want to soothe pain or other symptoms using color therapy.

COLOR DIAGNOSIS

Color changes in the body may be a sign of improved or of failing health. When a pink glow returns to the pale cheeks of a sick person, we know that person is well on the way to recovery, whereas if he or she is permanently flushed, we suspect the existence of a circulatory problem or raised temperature. Both complementary healing and some forms of mainstream medicine use the color of the skin as an indication of potential health problems. Possible skin diagnoses include yellow or orange skin signifying liver trouble; graying skin suggesting a depleted immune system; red, greasy skin showing heart or circulatory disorders, or fever; greenish skin indicating liver problems; and white patches showing kidney or liver trouble.

TONGUE COLOR

Advocates of traditional Chinese medicine believe that the color of the tongue–as well its texture, shape, and coating–reveal detailed information about a patient's health. A very pale tongue indicates fever, whereas a dark-red or purple tongue is a sign of possible heart trouble.

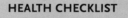

HEALTH CHECKLIST

If you want to improve one aspect of your physical, mental, or spiritual health, consult the list below for helpful colors.

If you suffer from poor concentration, consider using yellow or violet.

If you suffer from shortness of breath, consider using blue.

If you suffer from feeling the cold, consider using red.

If you suffer from indigestion, consider using yellow.

If you worry about or suffer from love problems, consider using orange.

If you are suffering from bereavement, consider using pink or green.

If you worry about or suffer from stress, consider using green.

If you suffer from persistent headaches, consider using blue or violet.

CHAKRAS AND BODY SYSTEMS

Each main chakra in the body is associated with a particular color and with a set of organs and a body system.

Chakra	Color	Organs	Body system
base	red	kidneys	muscular system
sacral	orange	reproductive organs and stomach	reproductive system
solar plexus	yellow	spleen, liver	digestive system
heart	green	heart	circulatory and nervous systems
throat	blue	throat, lungs	respiratory system
brow	indigo	eyes, ears, nose	skeletal system
crown	violet	brain	central nervous system (brain and spinal cord)

TREATING COLOR IMBALANCES IN THE BODY

There are many ways to use color to soothe aches and pains, protect organs or glands, or boost a body system.

Wrap colored scarves around an aching area, or on the part of the body where the organ is found.

Drink water energized with the appropriate color (see pages 132–35).

Rub color-energized water on an affected area.

Use colored light treatments (see pages 128–9).

Wear gemstones in the appropriate color.

Choose clothes in restorative colors.

Redecorate part of your home in the color you feel you need.

Channel the appropriate color (see pages 138–9) onto the affected part of the body.

Use color meditation to address areas of health concern (see pages 130–31).

Write color affirmations (see page 139) for a particular part of the body.

ZODIAC COLORS

Color theory ascribes colors to each sign of the zodiac. An intense attraction to or need for a particular color may be explained by your star sign.

Aquarius (Jan 20–Feb 17)
electric blue

Pisces (Feb 18–Mar 19)
turquoise, purple, green

Aries (Mar 20–Apr 19)
red

Taurus (Apr 20–May 20)
green

Gemini (May 21–June 20)
yellow

Cancer (June 21–July 22)
white, silver

Leo (July 23–Aug 22)
gold

Virgo (Aug 23–Sept 22)
light green, pale yellow

Libra (Sept 23–Oct 22)
blue, pink

Scorpio (Oct 23–Nov 21)
black, wine red

Sagittarius (Nov 22–Dec 21)
purple, magenta

Capricorn (Dec 22–Jan 19)
deep blue, deep green, black

light treatments

UNIVERSAL LIGHT

Observations of space indicate that the light in the universe is growing redder as it ages. Younger stars emit light at the blue end of the spectrum, but as stars grow older, their light shifts toward red. As the number of older stars in the universe increases, the predominant color of starlight moves from blue to red.

Light from very distant stars takes many millions of years to reach Earth—when today's astronomers observe a star, they see it as it was in the distant past, when the light began its long, long journey to Earth. In 2003 observations from the European Space Observatory telescope in Chile showed that 2.5 billion years ago, when the universe contained a larger number of younger stars, the light was predominantly blue.

Our bodies are sensitive all over to light. The energy of different colored lights can be absorbed through the skin as well as through the eyes (see page 12). In colored-light treatment we use our knowledge of the healing and balancing effects of colors to ease troublesome states of mind or to soothe aches and pains.

Colored-light treatments are given using the three primary colors of light: blue/violet, green and red/orange. Some treatments alternate a color with its complementary hue in a pair that is energizing/soothing (for information on complementary colors, see page 14). This alternation boosts the beneficial effect of the treatment.

BATHING IN LIGHT

You can feel the benefits of different colored-light treatments by "bathing" the body all over in a particular color. One way to do this is to combine a light treatment with a bath and to use colored bath foam as well as colored candles to achieve the required "all-over" effect.

You can also use colored bulbs or ordinary bulbs with colored filters to direct light of the required color onto the area of the chakra associated with the physical symptom or spiritual malaise that you are seeking to treat (see pages 120–21 and page 126). Either remove clothing from the chakra you are focusing on or wear white garments–otherwise, your clothes will filter the colored light and your body will receive a light treatment that combines the original color with that of your shirt or lower garments.

CHROMOTHERAPISTS

You can give yourself home treatment using colored light, but it is usually advisable to visit a trained color therapist or expert in colored-light treatment, known as a chromotherapist, for a session. Chromotherapists are trained in the use of specialized equipment and can offer light therapy delicately attuned to your particular needs.

THE COLOR OF LIGHT

Color therapists often split the primary colors of light into their constituent parts: red, orange, violet, blue, and green. Some add treatment with yellow light.

red light (base chakra)
Associated with vitality and strength; it can be used to treat lethargy and sometimes sexual impotence and (in addition to conventional medical treatment) to help with low blood pressure.

orange light (sacral chakra)
Associated with uplifting energy and happiness; orange light can be used to lift the spirits and improve a depressed state of mind.

violet light (crown chakra)
Boosts hope and a person's sense of inner worth and dignity; violet light treatment can be used to help people suffering from low self-esteem.

blue light (throat chakra)
Promotes relaxation and opening out; for this reason it is used with some success to ease the symptoms of asthma and migraine, and may also help if you are suffering from insomnia.

green light (heart chakra)
Associated with balance; it is used to clear muddled thinking and as a purifying force.

yellow light (solar plexus chakra)
Associated with intellectual activity and critical thought; yellow light treatment has beneficial effects in treating mental confusion. Therapists also report success treating rheumatism and arthritis with yellow light.

color meditation

Color meditation draws on the healing power of the color vibration that attracts your body or spirit. That color vibration is present in the light around you and can be drawn through your aura and chakras into your body to support organs and body systems, feed your life force, and elevate your spirit. Through the power of focused thought in meditation, you energize your body to receive the color.

If you have a physical illness or discomfort associated with an organ or body system, use the list on page 126 to identify the relevant chakra and its color. If you are suffering from low spirits or are trapped by emotions or bad habits, use the lists on pages 119, 121, 125, 129, and 134 to find the color you need. Practice meditation using that color. Persevere with the color meditation until you feel its benefit. Try to begin the meditation with a trusting and receptive attitude, with readiness to receive guidance and healing.

The effectiveness of positive thinking can be enhanced by color meditation. If you feel yourself slipping into negative, self-obsessed cycles of thought, use a burst of orange or yellow color meditation to energize and clarify your thought processes, or a burst of violet color meditation to strengthen your sense of connection with other people and your capacity to take pleasure in the happiness of others. Try a green color meditation if you are seeking the middle way between extremes.

ORANGE COLOR MEDITATION

Imagine that you are suffering from feelings of listlessness, you cannot summon up enthusiasm for your work, you feel reluctant to go out and meet friends. You decide to try a meditation in the color orange.

Sit comfortably in a position that allows you most easily to forget your body. If you practice yoga and are supple, you may choose to sit in the lotus position—on the floor, with your back straight, your legs crossed and each foot resting on the opposing thigh with the sole turned upward. Otherwise, sit in a straight-backed chair that encourages you to hold your spine erect and place your hands loosely on your thighs or along the arms of the chair, with palms turned up to indicate that you are receptive.

Imagine a sky of tender, delicate blue (complementary to orange), in which you see a sun of warming orange light. Alternatively, visualize a pool of peaceful blue on which you see floating a lotus of wonderful orange hue.

In this place, where you are entirely alone, the sun (or the lotus) manifests for you, makes its energy available for your healing. Its spinning orange center fills your field of vision as it draws you in. A cloud of orange warmth envelops you. You are in the scene and yet remain within yourself–all is unity.

At the heart of the cloud, where you are now seated, is a place of healing and blessed calm. In that place, your body finds perfect rest and the restorative energies that it needs, while your spirit is emboldened to understand your true nature and your right task in life; inhibitions and anxieties melt away, and self-assurance and confidence return.

When you are ready, you emerge from the place of healing, grateful for its restorative energy. Open your eyes to return yourself to the day and its demands. Your confidence and vitality restored, you are ready to pass on the loving energy you have received through work, service, and interaction with others.

colored water treatments

When colored light shines through a liquid, the liquid takes on some of the light's color energy. One easy way to treat yourself with color energy is to drink or bathe in color-energized water.

COLOR-ENERGY DRINKS

The time-honored practice of drinking color-energized water or milk to promote wellbeing–which was well-established among the ancient Egyptians and in the Indian Ayurvedic tradition–is returning to popularity.

Use liquid filled with the power of color energy as a complementary treatment to ease minor conditions and physical pains or as a way of reinforcing spiritual qualities.

Start by filling a jug or tumbler made of colored glass with mineral water or filtered tap water; alternatively, use clear glass wrapped in colored plastic. Set the glassware in daylight for 20 minutes. It need not be sunny.

Sip the contents, focusing your mind on the spiritual qualities you wish to foster or the physical symptoms you want to ease.

ENERGIZED WATER AND ITS PROPERTIES

violet
is associated with modesty and will relieve a
racing pulse or anxiety.

indigo
is associated with purity and will relieve aching
eyes or headaches.

blue
is associated with calmness and honesty and will relieve
a sore throat or nausea.

green
is associated with contentedness and will relieve a
nasty shock and skin complaints.

yellow
is associated with clarity of expression and a positive outlook
and will relieve constipation.

orange
is associated with good humor and an outgoing approach,
and will relieve indigestion.

red
is associated with passion and energy, and will relieve
exhaustion or poor circulation.

COLOR BATHING

A color bath delivers an all-over treatment with soothing or uplifting energy. Mix the appropriate color using food coloring or natural dyes. (Make sure you use non-staining varieties.)

indigo or blue
when you feel overheated, are seeking wisdom, are preparing for spiritual practice, or are taking a few days' retreat from ordinary life.

turquoise or green
when you feel tense, need to help others find a solution to a difficult problem or need to make a decision.

yellow
when you feel muddled and unequal to a task or need to rediscover your cheerful outlook.

orange
when you feel downhearted and need to restore your sense of humor and pleasure in everyday life.

pink
when you feel ill at ease or need to forgive yourself or others.

red
when you feel that your emotions are repressed or stifled, or your willpower is failing.

COLORS OF LOVE

Are you are having a difficult time attracting a loved one or maintaining a relationship? Use color energy to develop affection and other positive qualities in yourself or in your lover.

To develop qualities in yourself, use color meditation, colored water treatments or colored light therapy—or simply surround yourself with the appropriate color in your clothes, garden, home décor, or diet.

Surround your lover with color energy by using color meditation while visualizing him or her, or by channeling colors onto him or her (see pages 138–39).

If you are at a stage that is "in between" relationships, use pink energy to bolster your self-esteem, orange to develop self-confidence, and blue to settle anxiety.

If your relationship is static or dying out, use red to recreate passion.

If your relationships repeat damaging patterns of behavior, use magenta for escape from past mistakes and for making a new start.

If your relationship suffers from a lack of honesty, use blue to heal rifts, recreate trust, and encourage integrity.

If past mistakes prevent you from being happy now, use pink to dissolve anger, magenta to escape the past, and green to bolster hope.

If your lover or partner refuses to discuss problems, use orange to help communication and blue to encourage straight speaking.

breathing *colors* in and out

Color breathing is a form of meditation that is given added power by the intensity of the subject's concentration on the physical process of inhaling and exhaling. You can use this practice to infuse yourself, body and spirit, with the healing power of color.

SENDING COLOR ENERGY

You can perform color breathing for yourself or on behalf of another person: when you are intending to direct color energy toward another person, hold them in the full light of your attention for a few moments before starting the breathing exercise.

COLOR BREATHING EXERCISE

Find a comfortable place to sit (see page 130). Breathe in deeply, holding each breath for a few moments before breathing out gently, noticing the sensations associated with each part of your inhalation and exhalation. Establish a pattern of deep, restful breathing.

Incorporate the color you need to complete the exercise: use the lists on pages 119, 121, 125–6, 129, and 134 when making your color choice.

BLUE BREATHING

Imagine that you are breathing in light blue, to try to bring peace to your troubled spirit. As you breathe in, visualize wide shafts of blue light being drawn toward you. Blue light enters your body through your throat chakra.

Your lungs fill slowly with the serenity of blue, and this gentle cooling energy spreads throughout your body by means of your bloodstream. Places where you tend to carry tension—such as your shoulders or lower back—relax at the touch of the serene power of blue.

The blue in your exhaled breath is very faint at first, but as your lungs fill up with blue, the breath you send out becomes rich in the color. You have an abundance of blue energy.

You feel anxiety evaporate as calm touches your spirit and you begin to trust in your capacity to cope with difficulties. You are filled with blue light, floating in the limitless expanse of that peaceful vibration.

As you prepare to return to your ordinary surroundings, gradually test your awareness of the extremities of your body: start by wriggling your fingers and toes, then move your wrists and ankles, and gently move your neck. Lean forward a little to stretch your back. Open your eyes: you have returned to the present, feeling newly at peace with the world, vibrant with the gentleness of blue, inspired to communicate with others and share blue's elevating, healing energy.

RAINBOW COLOR BREATHING

Seat yourself comfortably and breathe deeply. Settle into a pattern of smooth, regular breathing. Visualize each of the rainbow colors as you breathe them in through the appropriate chakra. Complete at least five deep inhalations and exhalations for each color.

Start with the base chakra. See red energy flooding into the lower torso through the base chakra at the bottom of your spine: it floods through your circulatory system, bringing warmth and strength to every muscle.

See orange energy flooding through the sacral chakra at your navel: the healthy orange vibration flows through your reproductive organs, spreads throughout your body, delivering joy and vitality.

Yellow floods through the solar plexus chakra in the middle of your back, warming and energizing your digestive system.

Your heart chakra lets soothing green light flood into your nervous system.

Blue light enters your throat chakra: your powers of self-expression are fortified.

Indigo light passes through the brow chakra, in your central forehead, strengthening your eyes and bringing mental order.

Violet pours into the crown chakra at the top of your head, sparking spiritual yearnings by touching you with the promise of enlightenment.

channeling and *color* affirmations

One way of treating pain or discomfort with color energy is to direct the color you need onto the affected part of the body through your hands or by the power of visualization and meditative thought. Color can also be used to improve psychological help by making color affirmations.

CHANNELING COLOR WITH THE MIND

When deciding which color energy to use, bear in mind that pain in one place can be a symptom of a wider problem or a misalignment elsewhere in the body. Take care to treat the cause rather than just the symptom. For example, neck pain may be associated with problems in the muscular system or in the alignment of bones.

Color therapy suggests that cooling blue energy helps in the relief of pain. You could treat neck pain by channeling blue onto the neck and also by directing red onto the base chakra (at the base of the spine), which controls the muscular system, and indigo onto the brow chakra between the eyes. The brow chakra governs the skeletal system.

Start by settling yourself in a comfortable position, then concentrate on your breathing and allow your restless thoughts to settle.

Envisage a cloud of the color you have chosen rising up and enveloping the area you wish to treat. Alternatively, imagine the chakra that governs the body system you are treating open to admit color. Feel the color vibration enter the body. Color bathes and enriches every cell. The color introduces the energy that was missing before, restoring balance to that part of your body and the system that governs it. Before you open your eyes, envisage yourself in a state of perfect health, surrounded by a glowing aura that reflects the balance of color energies you contain.

CHANNELING COLOR WITH THE HANDS

You can channel color through your hands onto your own body or onto someone else's body.

Ask the person to lie down on a divan or bed and channel color healing onto the affected part of his or her body.

Prepare carefully: wash gently, try to settle your thoughts and breathing, and envisage yourself–particularly your hands–as a conduit for healing. Find a comfortable seated position.

COLOR MASSAGE

If a friend is trying color channelling, you can help to make it even more effective by combining it with a massage.

As you give the massage, feel the color energy in your fingers and in the skin and body of the person you are massaging. Imagine that the area you are massaging is rich in the color you are transmitting.

Use the power of your concentration to banish pain and energy imbalances from that part of the body.

if you feel upset, your affirmation might be "Using green energy I will find security and balance."

if you feel afraid, your affirmation might be "By embracing red energy I will go forward with confidence in myself and without fear."

if you feel overexcited or unable to settle or relax, your affirmation might be "Blue energy calms me, allowing me to accept my lot and proceed with trust."

if you feel daunted by a difficult job, your affirmation might be "Through indigo I develop my intuition and creativity

When you have summoned the color energy you need, hold your hands over the part of the body that needs healing.

Feel the energy passing through your fingers onto and through the skin, bringing healing energy to every cell and tissue. If you or your subject are wearing clothing over that area, it should be white or neutral in color.

COLOR AFFIRMATIONS

When writing an affirmation we call on the qualities we desire for ourselves—for example, by writing "I am confident of my ability to deal with any setback," "I am at peace with myself," or "I honor my intuition and my ability to be creative." Affirmations energize and reinforce our better selves, keeping self-doubt and lethargy at bay. Color affirmations summon the qualities of particular colors into our lives.

PICTURE CREDITS

KEY: **a**=above, **b**=below, **r**=right, **l**=left, **c**=center.

3 *ph* Debi Treloar; 4a *ph* Caroline Arber; 4b *ph* Sandra Lane/cushion from Graham & Green; 11 © Goodshoot; 13 © Stockbyte; 15 Courtesy of the Color Wheel Company; 17 *ph* Dan Duchars; 18a *ph* Earl Carter; 18b ph Andrea Jones; 19a *ph* Pia Tryde; 19b and 20 *ph* Polly Wreford; 21b *ph* Pia Tryde; 22 *ph* Craig Fordham; 26 and 27 *ph* David Montgomery; 28 *ph* Polly Wreford/ Marie-Hélène de Taillac's pied-à-terre in Paris; 30 *ph* Debi Treloar; 31 *ph* Polly Wreford/ Marie-Hélène de Taillac's pied-à-terre in Paris; 32 *ph* Chris Bracewell; 33 *ph* Tom Leighton; 34 *ph* James Merrell; 36 *ph* Debi Treloar/ Susan Cropper's family home in London, www.63hlg.com; 37 *ph* Polly Wreford; 39 *ph* Debi Treloar; 41 *ph* Catherine Gratwicke; 42 *ph* Catherine Gratwicke; 43 *ph* Polly Wreford; 44 *ph* James Merrell; 45a *ph* Christopher Drake; 46 The home of designer Etienne Mery in Paris *ph* Winfried Heinze; Alan Williams/Richard Oyarzarbal's apartment in London designed by Urban Research Laboratory; 51 *ph* Debi Treloar/ Debi Treloar's family home in northwest London; 53 *ph* Chris Everard/An apartment in Paris designed by architects Guillaume Terver and Fabienne Couvert of cxt sarl d'architecture; 57 *ph* Ray Main/Seth Stein's house in London; 54r *ph* James Merrell/Sally Butler's house in London; 58 *ph* Daniel Farmer; 59 *ph* Alan Williams/Owner of Gloss, Pascale Bredillet's own apartment in London; 60 Andrea Luria and Zachary Feuer's house in Los Angeles designed by Studio Works, Robert Mangurian and Mary-Ann Ray *ph* Ray Main; 61 *ph* David Brittain; 62 *ph* Debi Treloar/Architect Simon Colebrook's home in London; 63 *ph* Andrew Wood/Rosa Dean & Ed Baden-Powell's apartment in London, designed by Urban Salon Ltd; 66–67 *ph* Jan Baldwin/David Gill's house in London; 68 *ph* Catherine Gratwicke/the brownstone in New York of Bonnie Young, director of global sourcing and inspiration at Donna Karan International; 69 *ph* Ray Main/Seth Stein's house in London; 70–71 *ph* Alan Williams/Alannah Weston's house in London designed by Stickland Coombe Architecture; 74 *ph* Francesca Yorke; 76 *ph* Andrea Jones; 75, 77 and 78 *ph* Melanie Eclare/Daphne Shackleton's garden in Co. Cavan, Ireland; 79 *ph* Melanie Eclare; 81 *ph* Andrea Jones; 82 *ph* Francesca Yorke; 83 *ph* Caroline Arber; 84l *ph* Andrea Jones; 84r *ph* Interior Designer Philip Hooper's own house in East Sussex *ph* Jan Baldwin; 85r Blooms of Bressingham; 86 *ph* Andrea Jones/Rowden Gardens; 87 *ph* Melanie Eclare/Elspeth Thompson's garden in south London; 88a and 88b *ph* Pia Tryde; 89 *ph* Melanie Eclare; 90a *ph* Pia Tryde; 90b *ph* Steve Painter; 92–93 *ph* Melanie Eclare; 94 and 95 *ph* Francesca Yorke; 96 *ph* Pia Tryde; 97 *ph* Pia Tryde; 98 *ph* Tara Fisher; 100 *ph* Pia Tryde; 101 *ph* Vanessa Davies; 102 *ph* William Lingwood; 103 *ph* Debi Treloar; 104 and 105a *ph* Francesca Yorke; 105b&c *ph* Peter Cassidy; 106a *ph* Peter Cassidy; 106b *ph* Alan Williams; 107 *ph* Craig Robertson; 108l *ph* Francesca Yorke; 108r *ph* Alan Williams; 109a *ph* Pia Tryde; 109b *ph* Caroline Hughes; 110 *ph* Pia Tryde; 111 *ph* Alan Williams; 112–113 *ph* Debi Treloar; 114 The Family home of Shella Anderson, Tollesbury, UK *ph* Debi Treloar; 116 *ph* Chris Everard; 119 *ph* Jan Baldwin; 122 *ph* Daniel Farmer; 123 © Science Photo Library; 124–125 *ph* Polly Wreford; 127 *ph* Polly Wreford; 128 *ph* Debi Treloar ;131 inset *ph* Polly Wreford; 132 *ph* Emma Lee;135 *ph* Jan Baldwin; 134 *ph* Winfried Heinze; 137 *ph* Polly Wreford; 138–139 insets *ph* Polly Wreford.

The publishers would like to thank all those people who allowed us to photograph their homes for this book.

BUSINESS CREDITS

Baileys Home & Garden
Whitecross Farm
Bridstow
Ross-on-Wye
Herefordshire HR9 6JU, UK
+ 44 (0)1989 561931
www.baileyshome.com

Blooms of Bressingham
Low Road
Diss
Norfolk IP22 2AB, UK
+ 44(0) 1379 688585

Dive Architects
Gästrikegatan 20
S-113 62, Stockholm, Sweden
+46 8 33 10 30
www.divearchitects.com

Douglas Stephen Partnership
134 Old Street
London EC1V 9BL, UK
+ 44 (0)20 7336 7884
www.dsparchitecture.co.uk

Emma Greenhill
egreenhill@freenet.co.uk

Fabienne Couvert
Guillaume Terver
cxt sarl d'architecture
12 rue Saint Fiacre
75002 Paris, France
+33 1 55 34 9850
www.couverterver–architectes.com

Fiona McLean
McLean Quinlan Architects
1 Milliners House, Riverside Quarter,
Eastfields Avenue, London,
SW18 1LP, UK
+ 44 (0)20 8870 8600
www.mcleanquinlan.com

Gong
wholesale@gong.co.uk
+44(0)7930 327 772
www.gong.co.uk

Graham & Green
4 Elgin Crescent
London W11 2HX, UK
+ 44 (0) 20 7243 8908
www.grahamandgreen.co.uk

Hogarth Architects
186 Dawes Road
London SW6 7RQ, UK
www.hogartharchitects.co.uk

Iden Croft Herbs
Frittenden Road, Staplehurst,
Kent TN12 0DH, UK
+ 44 (0)1580 891 432
www.uk-herbs.com

Nick Coombe Architecture
34B Sutherland Square,
London SE17, 3EE, UK
+ 44 (0)20 7924 1699
nick@coombearchitecture.com
www.coombearchitecture.com

Peter & Pam Lewis
Garden design, restoration
and management
Sticky Wicket
Buckland Newton
Dorset DT2 7BY, UK
+ 44 (0)1300 345 476

Rowden Gardens
Brentor
Nr Tavistock
Devon PL19 0NG, UK
+ 44 (0)1822 810275
www.rowdengardens.com

Sage and Coombe
Architects
12 Vestry Street,
New York, NY 10013, USA
+1 212 226 9600
www.sageandcoombe.com

Seth Stein Architects
Unit 115, 300 Kensal Road,
London W10 5BE, UK
+ 44 (0)20 8968 8581
www.sethstein.com

Urban Research Lab
74C Duxton Road,
Singapore 089533
enquiries@urbanresearchlab.com
www.urbanresearchlab.com

Urban Salon Ltd
16 Stannary Street,
London SE11 4AA, UK
+ 44 (0)20 7735 5327
www.urbansalonarchitects.com

USEFUL WEBSITES

www.colourtherapyhealing.com
A color therapy resource.

www.iac-colour.co.uk
International Association of Colour.
Founded by colour therapy pioneer Theo Gimbel

freespace.virgin.net/hygeia.north
Hygeia College in the North.
Colour therapy courses.

index